Indigenous Church Planting

A Practical Journey

Other books by Charles Brock

Leading a Bible Study By Indirect Methods

Good News For You

I Have Been Born Again, What Next?

Galatians, From Law to Grace

John, Behold the Lamb

Romans, the Road to Righteousness

Principles and Practice of Indigenous Church Planting

Let This Mind Be In You

Questions People and Churches Ask

Indigenous Church Planting

A Practical Journey

Charles Brock

Copyright 1994 Charles Brock

Published by
Church Growth International
13174 Owens Lane
Neosho, Missouri 64850

All rights reserved. No portion of this book may be reproduced in any way without the written permission of the publisher, with the exception of brief excerpts quoted in magazine reviews, etc.

ISBN 1-885504-27-6

To Doug, Chris, and Greg

Our three sons who brought joy and fun to our lives
as each in his own way enhanced our church
planting years in a foreign land.

TABLE OF CONTENTS

Preface
Introduction
My Call to Missions 16

Section I - PRELIMINARIES TO PLANTING

Motivation For the Journey 22
Absolute Essentials and Excess Baggage 28
Who Can Plant Churches? 43
What Are We Seeking to Plant? 49
Roles of Ministry For the Pastor and Church
Members 62
The Lifestyle of the Church Planter 68
The Church Planter and the Language 74
Concentration: This One Thing I Do 78

Section II - FOCUS BEFORE STARTING

Know Your Parameters and Determine Your
Objectives Before Starting 86
What Is an Indigenous Church? 89
Identify Your Target Before Firing 96
Finding a Place to Plant a Church 99
A Pause For Some Practical Questions 106
What Strategy and Methods Will I Use? 124
What Style of Leadership Will I Use? 133
What Do You Do When There Is Little or No
Response? 137

Clearance From Community Officials to Have
a Bible Study 146
Promotion and Invitations 148

Section III - THE CHURCH PLANTING PROCESS

The Pre-Salvation Stage 151
Salvation: The First Objective 154
One Technique Illustrated 163

Section IV - THE BIRTH OF A CHURCH

They Have Been Born Again, What Next? 196
The Second Objective Reached: The Birth
of a Church 201

Section V - POST BIRTH

After the Birth: Development 204
Leadership Training 214
Church Organizational Meeting 220
The Church Receiving New Members 222
How Does a Church Get a Pastor? 228
What Titles Do We Use When Referring to
Religious Leaders? 233
What Should We Do When There Is an Emergency
Need Within the Church Family? 238
How Can a Church Encourage Members to Reach
the Lost? 242

Section VI - THE CHURCHES IN FELLOWSHIP

The Birth of a Fellowship or Association 247

APPENDIX

Church Planting Process 262
Testimony Sheet 263
Bible Reading Calendar 264
Church Growth Definitions 265
Bible Study Materials For Church Planting and
Church Growth 271

PREFACE

I am convinced of a need for radical revision of the traditional concepts of church and ministry. Fresh, Biblical church planting will be made possible only with a corresponding Biblical theology. The theme of this book is indigenous church planting. This kind of church planting is as thrilling and as uncontrollable as the Holy Spirit of God. After many years of practicing indigenous church planting, I have a greater conviction that it is the only kind of church planting in which I would want to invest a life. As you read the contents of this book you will quickly see that the planter is of importance, but the key to success lies in proper dependence on the Word of God and the Holy Spirit. With these two in the forefront, it is easier and natural for the church planter to fade into the background as an instrument. This does not minimize the church planter, but it relieves him of struggling to win people and give birth to churches. His struggle consists of maintaining spiritual readiness and availability.

In this book there is an attempt to be very practical in many areas of the life of a church planter, whether he be a national or foreigner. Though there is one method of church planting detailed, there is no thought of suggesting this is the only viable method. Though I have not and would not recommend ignoring indigenous principles, I personally have used a great deal of flexibility and experimentation in methodology. Every church planter should know well and feel comfortable with one method which is reproducible by new converts.

It is with joy that I share some things I have learned from personal experience over more than three decades in pastoral and missionary life. With gratitude to God for allowing me to have many years filled with wonderful church planting experiences, I pray the Holy Spirit will use the contents of this book to bring glory to Christ through the birthing of many churches.

I am deeply grateful for the great contribution of my wife Dottie in editing this book. But even more I am thankful for a lifetime of partnership in the venture God has given us. She has been my constant encourager.

Charles Brock

Introduction

For 26 years my wife Dottie and I were church planters. The journey began when I was 18 years old. Our first church planting experience was in Pioneer, Missouri. The last four years in the United States was given to church planting under a working relationship with the Home Mission Board and the Texas Baptist General Convention. In 1971 we sailed for the Philippines where it was our privilege to be involved in church planting for 20 years.

When we first arrived in the Philippines, indigenous church planting principles were almost unheard of, at least we were never introduced to them. For the first twenty years of the life of the Philippine Baptist Mission the work had marched forth only as fast as money and personnel would allow. Heavy subsidy was practiced at almost every point. The idea of church and church building were so intertwined that it was not natural to think of one without the other. The concept of ministry was very professionalized. The term "church planter" was new. The title was "field evangelist," which was a catchall that allowed a person to do many good things and never plant a church.

Working in a developing, third world nation made a paternalistic mentality an easy trap to fall into. Fortunately, the Mission saw the patterns that hindered church growth. Radical changes were made allowing the churches to provide for their own needs through the tithes and offerings of the members. Financial resources were not taken away, rather they were rechanneled to be used more constructively. A new loan board was established to take the place of grants for purchasing land and buildings. Churches were allowed to care for their own pastors. Theological education by extension was introduced making it possible for more church leaders to get their training without leaving home. The work of planting churches became more focused. The title "field evangelist" was changed to "church planter." This new title was more descriptive of Pauline missions, and it was a measurable term. The primary task was planting churches.

The changes did not come easily for some of the missionaries, as well as for some of the nationals. But within the next five years church growth was greater than in all of the first 20 years of the Philippine Baptist Mission.

These changes came very early in our missionary career. I had felt very uncomfortable with the traditional approach to church planting and felt freed by the indigenous approach.

Since indigenous principles were almost unknown, it was not a surprise to find indigenous practice almost an unknown. This also meant Bible study materials designed for indigenous church planting had not been produced. During a period of more than a dozen years in actual church planting, the Lord led Dottie and me in the development of a set of Bible study materials. Today these have become an integrated system of materials designed for church planting. These are based on Biblical indigenous principles and known for their ease of use, simplicity and reproducibility.

None of the contents of this book are armchair speculations. I will be sharing what I have actually felt and experienced. At no point am I speaking for a foreign mission board nor a local one. My expressed views are not necessarily the ones held by my colleagues or mission organization. I must hasten to add that I feel very comfortable with the philosophy of the Foreign Mission Board SBC with which I have worked through the years, and I love and feel loved by fellow missionaries.

It has been many years since my first book on church planting was published by Broadman Press. This book is much broader, dealing with many more aspects of the life of the church planter and his work. The passing of time has not diminished my commitment to indigenous church planting, rather it has become stronger. Time has allowed me to witness nationals from many countries, including the United States, embracing these principles and joyfully expressing a new found freedom. There is something about indigenous church planting that brings out a new sense of selfhood and dignity.

I have shared with many in church planting seminars the need to embrace eternal, Biblical, indigenous principles and cling to them whether there is apparent victory or not. Methodology is something else. There is need for flexibility as circumstances change. Differing personalities must be taken into account in determining application. Methods are many; principles are few. Methods often change, but principles never do.

The setting for much of this book is the Philippines. However, I have found Biblical principles are universal. Around the world in every culture people are lost because of the sin of unbelief. Only the Holy Spirit can empower the sower and draw the lost. Only He can make men thirst and then satisfy through magnifying Christ as Savior and Lord in the life of the sinner set free. The simple Bible message is the answer for everyone. The unchanging and urgent task for every believer is the communication of this message. Some will be privileged to do it in church planting. There is no thrill greater than for a sinner saved by grace, inhabited by the Holy Spirit and sharing God's nature, to plant church after church which will live and reproduce. In this book I will share in detail one method of planting churches. Let it be clearly understood that I am not saying this is the only viable way or the best way for everyone. The method will not be greatly different from that used by many church planters around the world. Basics will be magnified. Reproducibility will be an always-present factor to consider. The simple method is reproducible by new converts in any culture when applied by committed believers.

Any success that I have had is due to the ever-present and powerful Holy Spirit and the beautiful Word of God. This is the known secret that we tend to take for granted. My prayer is that more people will come to realize that church planting is an open option for such a host of God's people, and that He will use this book to bring honor to Himself by the expansion of His Kingdom through the planting of churches.

My Call to Missions

God works in all the little details of life to lead His children to the place where He wants them to serve. I am aware that He was working in my life when I was a ten-year-old believer. My first exposure to foreign missions was in Royal Ambassadors, a missions organization in the church where my family and I were members.

Years passed and upon graduating from high school my dream was to be a special agent with the Federal Bureau of Investigation. That dream was well on the way to fulfillment when I was employed by the FBI, working by day and preparing to enter law school at night. God, however, had other plans for me that were not a part of my dreams. He called me very clearly and persistently to preach the Gospel. Being a shy person, this was the last thing on earth I wanted to do or thought I could do. In my weakness God gave me assurance that He was able and would be with me every time I stood in the pulpit. After a great struggle, I believed Him and surrendered. I became a pastor of a small church at the age of eighteen and continued pastoring throughout four years of college and three years of seminary.

It was toward the end of my college days that God began to prepare me for ministry as a foreign missionary. My wife and I and our three sons moved to a pastorate some 85 miles away from the seminary I planned to attend. It was a small country church that knew how to love young pastors. Less than a year before we moved into the parsonage a member of the church, a fine Christian lady, had died. She left some money in her will to be used for missions. Some time after we began our ministry at that church, there was a group of men being gathered to go to the Philippines on a preaching ministry. A pastor of a nearby large city church mentioned this crusade to one of the deacons of our church. Immediately this deacon realized this was the way the money that was left for missions should be used. I was asked if I was interested in going on this preaching tour and there was no doubt in my mind. I was still a senior in college, a hurdle to be dealt with. All my teachers were very cooperative, giving me related assignments. For one month I was to be preaching the Gospel in the Philippines and Hong Kong.

It was an exciting adventure. Being only 24 years old, I did not know I was not supposed to like the "native" foods. There was no culture shock, just excitement and joy.

Our first week was in a very remote area on Mindanao. During the week I met some very interesting people. I remember well Harold Matthews and Dr. Elbert Walker who brought us some apples and other fruit to relieve us from rice and more rice. Another very interesting man came into my life during this time. His name was Luis Espanola, a farmer by trade. He went everywhere with the visiting team. He had a very large family, yet he had time to be a bivocational pastor for several small churches. Our first meeting was in the town where he lived. At the end of the week the team was to go to another place a few hours away to our second week of meetings. Brother Luis said he would come to bid us farewell at the end of the second week. I did not take him too seriously because the distance was great and he would have to take public transportation.

At the end of the second week, our day for departure, we were prepared to board the old rough riding bus to make a five-hour journey to the nearest airport. Just minutes before time to leave, the wiry little Luis appeared. We sat around a table in a large living room and prayed together. In Luis' prayer he said something that stuck in my heart. He said, "Dear Lord, please send Brother Brock back to the Philippines." It was not such a strange prayer except he omitted the names of the other two men making up the team. Why didn't he pray for them in the same way? This did not leave me.

Back to the USA and on to seminary I went. Since three years of seminary were in front of me, there was not much need to worry about foreign missions now. But then came missions day at seminary. I felt the Lord speaking to me. I walked to the front at the time of decision and surrendered my life to go wherever the Lord led.

Upon my graduation from seminary, a friend began talking to us about the need for pastors in the northern states. This sounded good and we looked into it. Almost immediately we were called to a new church-starting opportunity in Minnesota.

We were very happy in that work and enjoyed the location. We concluded that the Lord was not really calling us to foreign missions, rather He just wanted us to be willing to go wherever He wanted us. We were glad it was in America.

It was an exciting four years that we served in starting a new church in Minnesota. But after a church was born and a new building was completed, my heart began to be pulled in other directions. We were not sure where the Lord was leading us; we hoped it would be back to Missouri where our families lived. Six hundred miles was a long way to live from other family members. We even put out some feelers but felt no definite leading to those places.

News from afar bothered me. Elbert Walker, the man who directed that crusade in the Philippines, died unexpectedly from a heart attack; a gap was left.

Then almost immediately other bad news came. A couple I had met and fellowshipped with a great deal while on the crusade had resigned their church in Texas to return to serve in the Philippines. They had completed missionary orientation and in January were driving to bid some family members farewell. The road was spotted with ice. A head-on collision took both their lives. Who would go in their place?

The Lord knew I was rebelling. We had a good church, our boys were attending a fine school within walking distance from our house. We knew that they might not have such opportunities on a foreign mission field. Our parents were not getting any younger, and their health was declining. These were the makings of our subconscious, and sometimes of our conscious, thoughts.

One night I had a dream, a dream as real as life itself. In this dream, in a twinkling of an eye, my mother and father-in-law both died. Then the Lord stood before me and said, "All right, big boy, you have stayed so that you can have them. Now they are gone. Now what are you going to do?"

Shaken by the dream, I got up and made my way up the stairs and down the hall to my office. At the desk I noted a magazine lying there. It was face down. From the back cover the bold, black headlines jumped out at me: "Most urgent need today in missions is for evangelists." Would you dare guess the name of the country given where the need was the greatest? It was the Philippines, of course.

That was enough. My wife and I talked about it and immediately contacted the Foreign Mission Board telling them of our sense of calling. Within a few months we were in orientation and then on our way to the Philippines.

We have drawn several conclusions since those days.

1. The greatest joy and contentment are found in the center of God's will.

2. The safest place on earth is the center of God's will.

3. Our children will always be under God's watch care if we, the parents, are in His will.

4. God will not call us to do anything for which He will not give sufficient strength.

5. Life is too short and eternity too long to live for self.

6. My wife realized a joy from sharing in our sons' education that she would never have known had we stayed in the States. In the task God made her more than able, even to the point of enjoying it.

7. Only the continuing, clear call of God would keep us on the mission field.

SECTION I

PRELIMINARIES TO PLANTING

Chapter 1

Motivation For the Journey

The moving of history and the galloping population demand that more of God's children give their lives to church planting. Countless multitudes sitting in the pew week after week have the capacity to be involved in planting new churches. The businessman, the teacher, the farmer, under the leadership of the Holy Spirit, can plant churches. This is the normal expectation for people who are of the Way.

There is no journey more exciting than spending a life planting church after church. There is no greater way for a person to make deep ripples throughout the waters of history, eternally affecting the lives of multitudes. As churches are planted people come to know the Lord of life. Some of these people will become movers of their own society. Churches are born which will plant other new churches. On and on it goes, and it starts when a committed person dares to give his life to the Lordship of Christ as a church planter.

We have the necessary tools—all the tools Paul had—to plant big and little churches, both rural and urban. May our faith propel us to lose ourselves in getting the job done. We do not have time for the frustration of getting involved with denominational political bureaucracy and infighting. The hour is urgent; men are lost; our time at the task is as fleeting as the dew at sunrise. Through God's grace we have the Word and the Holy Spirit. What more could we want? Our only viable option is to be confident and courageous in spreading His Kingdom through the birth of new churches. Tomorrow is ours because we are His. Let's begin the journey now.

In so many of life's journeys, motivation seems to be a lion's share of getting something done. This is certainly true in church planting. There are some basic things we would assume to be true in a person's life before he is ready to be used successfully in church planting. Briefly we will look at some of these as they relate to **motivation.**

Motivation comes from knowing where and how one fits into a winning team.

A church planter will be greatly motivated if he understands something of what God is about in the universe. A fuzzy concept of what God is doing through Christ will leave a planter frustrated and with little motivation. To catch a glimpse of God's eternal purpose and how man fits into it will carry the planter far down the church planting trail. You may respond, "Don't we all know this?" I am not so sure that a Biblical Christian world view has so lodged in the minds of the average would-be church planter that he naturally and spontaneously lives to expand God's Kingdom through the birth of reproducible churches.

From a personal involvement in God's plan of the universe, a church planter will see beyond the commonly held materialistic and humanistic world views to the excitement of seeing slaves set free—free to be what God has purposed each person to be. In his letter to the people in Colossae, Paul most clearly sets forth the Biblical world view that is worth living for. In Colossians 1:12-14 Paul says, *May you be made strong with all the strength which comes from his glorious power, so that you may be able to endure everything with patience. And with joy give thanks to the Father, who has made you fit to have your share of what God has reserved for his people in the kingdom of light. He rescued us from the power of darkness and brought us safe into the kingdom of His dear Son, by whom we are set free, that is, our sins are forgiven.* In verse 20 of that same chapter, Paul further states, *Through the Son, then, God decided to bring the whole universe back to himself. God made peace through his Son's death on the cross and so brought back to himself all things, both on earth and in heaven.* In verse 27 we read, *And the secret is that Christ is in you, which means that you will share in the glory of God.* In this concept the church planter finds himself a recipient of a tremendous privilege of sonship that will reflect in life the character of God as seen in Christ. The ensuing companion of this privileged position is the weighty responsibility of priesthood.

From such heights of experiential understanding of being inhabited by God, a planter can see the anguish of the sinner and yet visualize the potential of that person through Christ. Only as the planter becomes an active participant with God in redeeming the world will he have adequate motivation to push him from victory to victory. The planter knows that churches can be born which are indigenous, because with God as the source, any group of believers is capable of functioning as a family (church). The planting of self-governing, self-supporting, self-expressing, self-teaching, and self-propagating churches is not a far-fetched fantasy when the Christian world view becomes a living reality in the life of the planter. If it is alive in the planter's life, it will come alive in the churches he plants.

Motivation comes from knowing that people without Christ are eternally lost.

Universalism says somehow, someday, a loving God will get everyone to Heaven. The Bible says this is not true. John's gospel declares, *Whoever believes in the Son has eternal life: whoever disobeys the Son will not have life, but will remain under God's punishment.* John 3:36 God is not willing that any should perish, the Bible says. He provided a way, **one** way of escape. To by-pass the death, burial, and resurrection of Christ and build bridges composed only of religious rituals will surely leave a people hopeless and forever lost. Jesus spoke much of hell as the eternal abode of men who refuse God's plan of salvation. Jesus can be trusted. The church planter who never weeps over the lostness of mankind should cease calling himself a church planter. Those who see and weep will go forth. To the planter in such a position of compassion, God gives seed to plant and the harvest to gather.

Motivation comes from knowing God's Word is sharp enough to do the job.

The farmer who must work without adequate tools is hindered and may be discouraged. To go forth to plant churches without full confidence in the Word of God is as exciting and fruitful as the woodsman going to the forest without an ax. It is not man's word that is inspired, it is God's Word. It is not man's word that will convict, it is God's Word. A tongue of silver is nothing compared to the pure, faultless Word of God. The planter's personal confidence is measurable by his faith in the power of the Word. What God's Word says is more important than anything man has to say about God's Word. The church planter who knows this to be true is freed to rely on God's Word rather than on his own speech and knowledge. Confidence in the power of the Word will motivate the church planter.

Motivation comes from knowing that the Holy Spirit is more than theory.

To have the Holy Spirit actualized in the routines of daily life frees the church planter from loneliness and impotence. In church planting the Holy Spirit can do what money cannot do. He can do what a church planter cannot do. He can do what a polished organization cannot do.

In our day it is possible to plant even a big "church" without the presence or power of the Holy Spirit. I once heard a pastor of a large, thriving church say, "Our church machinery is so well oiled that the Holy Spirit could be gone a month before anyone noticed it." In an emotionally charged society, with the right charisma in a leader, whether it be of God or not, the result can be a large gathering of people. With a large dose of money, even a leader with less charisma may lure a crowd, especially in underdeveloped nations. This is possible with the Holy Spirit relegated to a respectable theological shelf.

It is interesting to study closely the secret of the rapid expansion of the early church in New Testament days. There were no classes on anthropology and communication. There were no committees trying to pry more money from local or foreign sources to buy land, rent a building, or pay a pastor's salary. They had no one with a doctorate in missiology. Their basic resources were: **commitment, the Holy Spirit, and the Word of God**. If a church planter would be free from frustration and discouragement, these three elements must be alive and foremost in his venture.

The Holy Spirit was the secret of effective communication in the New Testament. It was He, a living person with power, who miraculously effected deep communication. I am not suggesting that a church planter should ignore culture and language. He must be fully aware of culture and do his best to learn the language of the hearers. But this is not the primary key in communicating the Gospel. The Holy Spirit is the only one who can adequately open hard hearts to be receptive to the Word of God. The Holy Spirit can more easily use the planter who is committed and prepared. But the planter can be well prepared in human resources, yet ignore the supernatural work of the Holy Spirit.

The greater the reliance upon the three basic elements of New Testament church planting, a committed sower, the Word, and the Spirit, the more likely the birth of a genuine church. The Holy Spirit and the Scripture are the strings that draw and unite a group, if that group is really a church. The more the drawing and binding is attributed to anyone or anything other than the Word and the Holy Spirit, the more the group is suspect, even though it be called "church."

Motivation comes from knowing that one is called by God.

No one moves and speaks with authority as much as the person who is absolutely sure God has called him to a task. If God clearly calls a person to plant churches, that person will have confidence and motivation. Without a definite call, a person may be casual, without direction, just passing time. A clear, undiluted call compels a person to a revolutionary status because he has all the authority of the universe behind him.

The church planter who is there because of God's definite call will dream dreams. He can dare to have irregular thoughts and plans. All human weaknesses can become secondary in the light of God's call. God's call makes the weak strong, the timid bold. What would Jeremiah and Isaiah have been without God's call? How far would Paul have gone as a church planter without God's call? The call is not limited to one's education. It is not limited to one's skills. This is what God's grace and power is all about; He takes those who are weak and makes them strong. He takes common clay and makes it into something beautiful and useful. So He does with the church planter. To be called, to be chosen, is a factor that motivates. A strong sense of being called for church planting is the bedrock for finding handles, ways of doing it. The calling will result in searching for the most effective way of planting churches.

Chapter 2

Absolute Essentials and Excess Baggage

There are a number of critical issues which must be dealt with before one goes to a place to share the Gospel message. Bypassing or ignoring these critical issues would be like the farmer going to the field to work without prior thought or preparation.

Many years have passed since I wrote *The Principles and Practice of Indigenous Church Planting*. In that book I said there are four absolute essentials in church planting, the Seed, Spirit, Sower, and Soil. Today I am more convinced than ever that these are the four essentials which are indispensable. Caution must be observed when adding anything beyond these four essentials. Anything additional may be detrimental to healthy church planting.

When our three sons were still with us in the Philippines, we decided to take a trip through Europe on the way back to the States for furlough. For months we read travel guides and chose the places we would visit. We decided which sights we would see in each place. We determined the budget we would follow. We were trying for Europe on five dollars a day after the book *Europe on Ten Dollars a Day* came out. Before beginning the journey, we bought five travel bags which were small enough to be carried onto the plane with us. Each of us had our own and packed it about half full. Only the essentials were allowed. The trip was going to be three weeks so there was not a need for a large suitcase, that is if we wanted a carefree trip on a limited budget.

From the airport in Rome, we went by bus to the central train station in the city. Because of previous study, we knew the names and addresses of reasonably priced places of lodging. My wife and two of our sons sat down with the luggage at the station while our other son and I started walking, looking for a good place to stay for three or four days. After finding a place a few blocks away, we returned to the train station. Each member of the family picked up his own very lightweight bag and off we walked. After repeating this for three weeks all across Europe, we were glad we did not have excess baggage. Excess baggage would have meant two or three taxis from each airport. There would have been undue worry from having to watch more bags. There would have been the constant fear of having lost or delayed luggage on each flight. Fatigue from carrying heavy loads, extra time required at check in, and wasted time at luggage claim areas would have used up valuable time and energy we needed for seeing the interesting sights. Had we, like typical Americans, taken five to ten big suitcases (excess baggage) the trip would have been much tougher, much more expensive, and much less enjoyable.

Excess baggage can be a major problem in church planting. It may include concepts and programs, as well as the use of material things. To carry things beyond the essentials will tend to be excess baggage.

The four essentials are clearly seen in the life of Paul, the master church planter. We see them in I Thessalonians 1:5: *For we brought the **Good News to you**, not with words only, but also with power and the **Holy Spirit**, and the complete conviction of its truth.*

In Romans 15:18-19a we see the four again. *I will be bold and speak only about what Christ has done through **me** to lead the **Gentiles** to obey God. He has done this by means of **words** and* *deeds, by the power of miracles and wonders, and by the power of the **Spirit** of God.*

I have used bold print to point out the four essentials in Pauline missiology. In I Thessalonians it was **we,** this is the **Sower; Good News,** this is the **Seed; you,** this is the **Soil; Holy Spirit,** this is the **Spirit** that pervades the church planting experience from beginning to end if it is to succeed.

The four essentials for all church planters are: Spirit, Seed, Sower, Soil. Without any one of these, New Testament church planting is impossible. On the other hand, anything added to these may tend to be excess baggage that could deter effective church planting. The common access to the essentials makes church planting a possibility for more people than generally thought. Churches can be planted without big finances or elegant buildings. Churches can be planted by ordinary people who are filled with a vision and the Holy Spirit. The secret is no longer bound to a religious title or degree. The necessary resources are available to multitudes. Let us look more closely at the four essentials.

The first essential in church planting is the Holy Spirit.

The book of Acts has been described in many ways. Some call it the Acts of the Apostles, others say it is an unfolding of the early church, an expansion of Christianity. Still others say it is an account of the Acts of the Holy Spirit. All may be right to some degree. For sure, one cannot escape the dominating presence and power of the Holy Spirit in the unfolding story of the march of faith from one region to another.

Note a few selected passages from Acts concerning the Holy Spirit:

1:8 *But when the Holy Spirit comes upon you, you will become . . .*
2:4 *They were all filled with the Holy Spirit . . .*
4:8 *Peter full of the Holy Spirit, answered them, . . .*
4:31 *They were all filled with the Holy Spirit . . .*
6:10 *But the Spirit gave Stephen such wisdom . . .*
8:29 *The Holy Spirit said to Philip . . .*
10:19 *. . . the Spirit said, "Listen! . . .*
11:15 *The Holy Spirit came down on them . . .*
13:2 *The Holy Spirit said to them, Set apart for me Barnabas and Saul, . . .*
13:9 *Then Saul—also known as Paul—was filled with the Holy Spirit; . . .*
15:28 *The Holy Spirit and we have agreed . . .*
16:6 *The Holy Spirit did not let them preach the message in the Province of Asia.*
20:22 *And now, in obedience to the Holy Spirit I am going to Jerusalem.*
20:23 *. . . the Holy Spirit has warned me . . .*

From beginning to end, our source of strength and wisdom comes from the indwelling Holy Spirit. He goes before us in opening doors and preparing hearts. It was not human wisdom or strategy that sent Philip in the heat of the day to a dusty road to meet someone he did not know. This type of event is not foreign or unusual for the modern day church planter who knows the leadership of the Holy Spirit. Extensive surveys are a part of my life as a church planter and the study of maps and population trends are a normal part of my approach to church planting. But I must emphasize that if all of my fruit is the result of such human studies, I have missed the mark and the corresponding walk with God that Paul knew. The Holy Spirit still is in the business of saying, "Get up and go to a place where I will show great and mighty things that only God can produce." Sometimes we feel uncomfortable around a person who says, "The Holy Spirit told me to do it." But is this not exactly the tenor of the New Testament? The Bible admonishes us to "walk in the Spirit" and "pray without ceasing." This can be an exciting reality for a church planter. The trip is not worth it unless this is a primary part of the package.

After serving in rural areas as a church planter for ten years, the Lord led us to transfer to Manila. Our assignment was Quezon City, a large city at the northeast side of Manila. We had a new church born in an affluent subdivision, and I noted there was a second phase of the subdivision a few miles away. Beautiful houses were springing up daily. Time after time I went to the area and mingled with the people, looking for any contact the Holy Spirit had prepared. I wanted to start a new church in that place. One day as I was sitting in my car observing and praying, I noticed across a valley what appeared to be a large community beyond a river. Day after day I went there, visiting people wherever I found them. To the health clinic, to the barrio captain's house I went, but it seemed the time was not right. On another day when I was in the developing subdivision, praying, looking across the river to the large community, I noticed something else happening. Across another valley there were many new houses popping up along a mountain top. They were thatch-roofed squatters' houses. One could actually be built in a day. Week after week I observed the development of a new squatters' village stretching across the mountain ridge.

One day I felt a strong compulsion to try to find a way to the village. I drove as close as possible and then began the hike down a hill, across a valley, and over to the top of the mountain. As I began walking down the hill, before my eyes appeared a large community of people in the valley. The houses, sheltered by the trees, had not been visible to me before. Just to my right I saw a house tucked against the hillside with a man cleaning his yard. We exchanged greetings. He asked, "Where are you going?" I answered, "Across to the new houses on the mountain." To be friendly, he asked me what I was going to do there. I told him I was a Bible teacher and was going there to see if there was someone who wanted to study the Bible. He said, "We have been waiting for you to come." I thought, how can this be, we have never met. He said, "Let's go down to meet the barrio captain; he will be interested." When I met the captain he said, "We have been praying that you would come."

Does the Holy Spirit still lead beyond our wildest expectations? I say without a doubt, He does. It was not an accident that within three to four months a good church was born when 36 new believers were baptized. Immediately the members shared in the teaching, preaching, and singing responsibilities. Within a year they had built a chapel with their own money and manpower. They chose to call themselves the Grace Church because God had been so gracious to them. The Holy Spirit was adequate to lead to the right place, call the people out, equip them for ministry, and guide them in outreach.

The secret of successful church planting and church growth is found in Acts 9:31. *And so it was that the church throughout Judea, Galilee, and Samaria had a time of peace. Through the help of the Holy Spirit it was strengthened and grew in numbers, as it lived in reverence for the Lord.*

The second essential is the Word of God, the Bible.

*How wonderful it is to see a messenger coming across the mountains, bringing **good news**, the news of peace!* Isaiah 52:7 Also in Isaiah 55:10-11 we hear the beautiful words, ***My word** is like the snow and the rain that comes down from the sky to* *water the earth. They make the crops grow and provide seed for planting and food to eat. So also will be the **word** that I speak—**it will not fail** to do what I plan for it; **it will** do everything I send it to do.*

I have used bold print to emphasize the place of the Word and the positive nature of its power. There is no question about its power. Paul had full confidence in the Word. He said, *I am eager to preach the Good News . . . I have complete confidence in the gospel; it is God's power to save all who believe . . . The Gospel reveals how God puts people right with Himself . . .* Romans 1:15-17

It is vital for the church planter to believe that *All Scripture is inspired by God . . .* II Timothy 3:16. Anyone who must pick and choose, using human wisdom to decide which part of the Bible is God's Word and which part is only man's word will have a difficult time planting Bible-principled churches.

While I was leading a church planting seminar in Dallas, Texas, a young man asked me if I had ever been discouraged in church planting. I had to pause and think about it because it had never entered my mind. Finally I told him that, as far as I could remember, I had never been discouraged in church planting. Perhaps it sounded strange because I know I am not a super human or super saint. There was nothing within my strength or ability to make such a claim. I began to think about it more. There had been times of homesickness, frustration, and impatience with a culture that sometimes makes no sense to the American mind. But I could not recall ever having been discouraged. The secret is seen in the life and writings of Paul. *We say this because we have confidence in God through Christ. There is nothing in us that allows us to claim that we are capable of doing this work. The capacity we have comes from God; it is He who made us capable of serving the new covenant, . . .* 2 Corinthians 3:4-6a

Hear the model church planter when he says, *God in His mercy has given us this work to do, and so we do not become discouraged.* 2 Corinthians 4:1 Again he says, *For this reason we never become discouraged.* 2 Corinthians 4:16

Paul was commissioned and committed to preaching the pure Gospel. He said concerning preaching the Gospel, *After all, I am under orders to do so. And how terrible it would be for me if I did not preach the gospel!* 1 Corinthians 9:16

Paul was assured of victory and could never be discouraged because he was fully aware that . . . *the gospel I preach is not of human origin.* Galatians 1:11 He went on to say, *I did not receive it from any man, nor did anyone teach me. It was Jesus Christ himself who revealed it to me.* Galatians 1:12

The church planter has only one book that is authoritative, and the closer he sticks to that book, the Bible, the greater his success will be. As I look back across the years and remember how God's Word implanted in the hearts of unbelievers gradually brought them to understanding and conviction, and finally conversion, I know why I was never discouraged. But the moment we minimize the Word and seek to use our own wisdom and persuasiveness, we are headed down the road to discouragement. It is strange how we sometimes seek to enhance the Word of God. Wise is the planter who can rest and relax, permitting the Word to speak. The Word is more than adequate in its own power. We must remember that what God's Word says is more important and more powerful than anything we can say about it.

Years ago when working in a northern province of the Philippines, I would go out nearly every night to lead church planting Bible studies. In rainy season, driving was always hazardous. The narrow, black paved roads were so black when the rain was falling. The narrow bridges often made the meeting of speeding buses and trucks a death-defying stunt. The near misses made me so aware that a few inches closer and I would never reach home alive. One day I told my wife, "If some night one of those buses gets too close and I don't make it, you will know I died singing." That is the life of a church planter who has full confidence in the Word. Week by week, as the Gospel seed was sown in the lives of the unbelievers, I could see so clearly the gradual opening of the eyes of their understanding. It was not a big thing, but enough to assure that God was doing something through His Word. Watching unbelievers inch toward new life brings a song to the sower's heart.

The faithfully sown Word never leaves people untouched. It makes a difference. The Word is powerful. It never leaves a person the same. He either moves farther away from God or nearer.

Many years ago I traveled to a nearby province where I was going to experiment with having five or six Bible studies from early morning until evening. Out of these Bible studies my goal was one or two new churches. Normally I have a lesson each week, but these were to be daily within a one-week period. So from one place to the next I went all day Monday through Friday. The people were farmers and fishermen. The response was good with a good attendance for each of the studies. By the end of the series of studies, a number of people made professions of faith in Christ. I told them that after three weeks or so, I would return to meet with each group to talk to them about their new life.

When I returned I went to the first barrio and drove to the place where we had met for the Bible study. Normally, if a foreigner went there in any vehicle, out of curiosity many people would come out to meet him. On this day no one was in sight. I waited for a good while and finally an old man came out and ashamedly told me that the religious leader of the community had told all of them never to talk with me again. If they did, their children could no longer attend school. (In that area the schools were under the direction of religious leaders.) I went to the next barrio. Again, I went to the place where the group had met under a tree. No one appeared for a long time. At last a young man came out with the same message I had received at the previous place. He offered to return the New Testament I had given him as an appreciation gift for hosting the Bible Study. He said "I cannot keep this book, and we cannot listen to you anymore." I had felt optimistic about this group. A number of young adults had made what had appeared to be genuine decisions to follow Christ. I told him I could not accept the Bible; it was his. He insisted on giving it to me. I told him it was God's Word to us and that it told the way of new life here and how to go to heaven when we die. I took the little brown limber New Testament and said, "I will never take this book with me. You must decide what you will do with it." I asked for a match and he gave me one. I opened the Bible and laid it on the ground, struck the match and said, "This is your decision." As the flame neared the pages, the wind blew out the flame. (I felt relieved. I was not in the habit of burning Bibles.) I asked for another match and the young man gave me one. He became anxious as he realized I was serious about burning the Bible. Again, the match was struck. As the flame neared the page the young man grabbed the book and clutched it saying, "I will keep it!" (I am not suggesting that we go around burning Bibles to try to prove a point, but I felt an urging of the Holy Spirit to do this as a dramatization of the reaction of these people to the Word of God.) The Bible is powerful and meaningful. It never leaves a person undecided. Indecision is a negative decision. Wherever the Bible goes it touches and affects lives. It is not an ordinary book; it is God's Word! In our hands we have a Living Book. Paul claims it to be "alive, active, and sharper than any two-edged sword."

In my church-planting experience it has been normal to hear church members say, "Thank you for bringing the Good News to us." Often these would be people with little money and earthly possessions. Yet, out of gratitude they would give us bananas or whatever fruits or vegetables they had. They were so thankful that someone loved them enough to bring them something of greater value than financial aid. I found that where missionaries had first gone in with financial assistance, the people tended to become dependent, having the mentality of "What do you have for us today?" The Gospel produces a dignity beyond beggarhood. If our primary message is not the Gospel, we have no message of eternal consequence. God has given us the thing people need most. It is the Seed that must be planted and nurtured.

The Psalmist was right when he said, *Your word, O Lord, will last forever; it is eternal in heaven.* Psalms 119:89

The third essential in church planting is the sower.

Church planting is a choice way to spend a life. God has chosen to use finite men and women to be His instruments in planting churches. There is no joy greater than that of seeing churches planted which will live on and on. There is no greater way to impact history than by planting churches. There is no better way to help people socially and economically than by planting churches. There is no greater way to love people than through planting churches.

Paul thought it worth a lifetime of tireless energy, persecution, and even death. He was a man aware of a mission, a mission of life and death for his people. He said, *My conscience, ruled by the Holy Spirit, also assures me that I am not lying when I say how great is my sorrow, how endless the pain in my heart for my people, my flesh and blood! For their sake I could wish that*

I myself were under God's curse and separated from Christ.
Romans 9:1-3

He said, *My brothers, how I wish with all my heart that my own people might be saved! How I pray to God for them!* Romans 10:1 He saw the link, the essential link of the church planter when he said, *And how can the message be proclaimed if the messengers are not sent out? As the Scripture says, "How wonderful is the coming of messengers who bring Good News!"* Romans 10:15

If God has called a person to be a church planter, what a pity if that person should stoop to become the president of a nation. It is a high and holy calling with a heavy responsibility. It is not a way of life to be entered into lightly or for any reason other than the clear, inescapable call of God. The harvest is dying on the vine due to a lack of church planters. The need is not just one church in a city, but local autonomous churches within the easy reach of every person. The Kingdom will multiply through the birth of churches. How shall they be planted without planters?

The fourth essential in planting churches is the soil, the people.

The Bible talks about the different kinds of people—those who have hardened hearts, those whose hearts allow the things of the world to become a barrier to the Gospel, and those who are thirsty for the Good News. It is the responsibility of the church planter to be among the people with a full awareness of the kinds of soil around him.

The planter must be aware that all people without Christ are lost and need a Savior. When the planter sees the multitudes today, there should be the same concern as when Jesus saw the multitudes in Jerusalem and grieved. There is no substitute for being among the people if we would plant churches. It is not done in a classroom or in an office. The field is the world, and the world is the people. There is the saying, "There's just so much land, and no more is being made," but concerning people, multiplication is going on. We face the danger of church planting experiencing addition rather than multiplication.

What are some things which may be excess baggage?

Money, gadgets and things may be excess baggage but concepts and theological positions may be just as great a hindrance to church planting. Some of these concepts or ideas are:

1. The idea that a church that meets in a church house is more genuine than a church that meets in a home.

2. Singular leadership in the new church.

3. The idea that Northerners will flock to meet with a click of southern transferees.

4. Predicting the future on the basis of past resistance or failures. This requires no faith at all.

5. The idea that if one sector of society is resistant then all others must be.

6. A flawed definition of what a church is.

7. The idea that only the professional clergy can be effective church planters.

8. Low expectation level for new believers.

9. The idea that if a church ceases to function as a group, the church or planter is a failure.

In our increasingly mobile society we must understand that people-oriented churches will differ from churches which are land, building, and program oriented. A church may be needed in a certain area for only five or ten years. Transition of population may mean that a church is no longer needed or practical in that location. The transferring of members to different locations may mean the group will cease to meet as a local church. This is not failure.

Seldom will a church die, but I have seen churches disperse and multiply themselves. In Metro Manila we had this happen to one of our new churches. It was a small group, but most of the members were committed believers and were growing in their Christian walk. There was a very close family relationship in the group and a common concern for family and friends who had not yet come to know the Lord. In the second year of the church's existence, the core members were suddenly transferring to other areas.

The family in whose carport we met sold their house and moved about two hundred miles to the north of Manila. They went with a commitment to start a new church in their new home town where Bible believing churches were rare.

Another key member felt God calling her to go to Kuwait to share the Gospel. She went as a medical technician, but her goal was to share the Gospel. She was commissioned and sent out with the prayer support of the newly formed fellowship of churches in northeast Manila.

Two other very dedicated young women transferred to Chicago and became active in outreach there.

Another young woman felt God calling her to tribal missionary work. She went to work among the tribes of northern Luzon as a full-time church planting missionary with New Tribes Mission.

A young man was instrumental in beginning and developing a large church in Manila.

Another talented young woman married a preacher and now serves the Lord as the dedicated wife of a pastor.

Others scattered and, as far as we know, all of them are very active in church planting or church growth. The church ceased to meet as a group but there was no failure.

While we must be on guard against excess baggage, we must keep uppermost in our minds the basic essentials. It is important to always keep in mind Paul's model in church planting. He stayed with the basic essentials and the Lord blessed his efforts. The essentials were and continue to be: The Holy Spirit, the Seed, the Sower, and the Soil.

Chapter 3

Who Can Plant Churches?

Some people have the very erroneous idea that only a preacher can start churches. Some would think one must have seminary training in order to plant churches. Also, these would usually think that one must have a public ordination ceremony before being qualified to plant churches. It is amazing how man-made, extra-Biblical tradition can come to the place of being considered sacred. All of the above ideas about who can plant churches have arisen from religious/political sources.

There is no doubt that to be ordered (ordained) of God to plant churches is a primary prerequisite for the church planter, but to demand that one ritual which has developed in one part of the world is to be applied to all of the world is a little far-fetched. It is the inner, personal ordination between God and the person which is of primary importance. However, it can often be of value to have a recognition of ordination service. This public service can vary from a long, ritualistic ceremony to a simple announcement and recognition of the fact. But one can be very successful in planting churches even when there is never a formal public ordination service or recognition of such. Winston Crawley, a leading missiologist has said, "We have to get away from the feeling that the preacher must do it all, and that we can't carry on a worthy program unless he has been to seminary. How subtle it is—this idea that everything centers in a building and a seminary-trained leader, and unless you have those two, evangelism can't go forward. . . . I doubt that you will find that subtle idea in the New Testament. Some way we must break away from this pattern." (From Missionary Intercom, 1974)

As long as we are bound by the tradition that only those who have been to seminary or Bible school can effectively plant churches, the world doesn't have a chance. Biblical history and current experience reveal that more people can be effective in planting churches than many would dare believe.

Some of the most effective church planters in the New Testament were people with varying backgrounds and qualifications. Some would call Aquila and Priscilla only laypeople, but they were used mightily in the establishment of the work in Ephesus. Apollos, a strong preacher, was used in the beginning and development of new churches. Barnabas, perhaps not such a great preacher but an encourager/teacher had a great impact on the Antioch church. Timothy, Titus and Tychicus participated in planting and developing churches. I have known many effective church planters who have pastoral training and experience. However, such training and experience are not the primary qualifications of an effective church planter.

One of the most effective church planters I know is a young woman in the northern part of the Philippines. When my family went to the Philippines, our three sons were small and my wife had the privilege of teaching them at our home. Because of this heavy load and for a number of other reasons, we found it imperative to have a helper in the home. The Lord led us to Miss Victoria Gapuz. Vicky was a convert from the very strong cultic, indigenous religion called Iglesia ni Cristo. Not only was she a good helper in the home, she was also teachable in the ways of church planting. On a regular basis I would share ideas and get her opinion about various techniques and approaches in church planting. She soon understood and appreciated the indigenous approach as much, if not more than I. Each weekend she went home to her barrio. She lived along the South China Sea coast in a tobacco-growing community. It was not long before she started a Bible study among her friends and neighbors. Within a year a new church was born. She continued to guide the church and train new leaders. After a few years that church bought its own land and built its own place of worship—all without outside financing or loans. Today the church is pastored by a seminary graduate. Who can plant churches? This was just a beginning for Vicky. After a few years, we had transferred to another area and left the leadership of the association in the hands of a Filipino, a seminary-trained young man. The association of churches took care of his salary. When he left to go to another pioneering area, with full confidence in Miss Gapuz, the association of churches elected her as their new association missionary and church planter. When we left the Philippines several years later, she was still giving outstanding leadership to the association and planting new churches every year.

At a church-planting seminar a few years ago in Cebu City, Philippines, it was interesting to see that among the 100 present, some of the outstanding church planting testimonies came from young women. (These were not assuming the role of a pastor/preacher.)

Tom Escota, a businessman in Manila, is one of the most effective church planters I have ever met. Tom began pastoring a new church six months after he was saved. Within two years he replaced me as missions director and church planter of the association in Quezon City. He was not a college graduate nor a Bible school or seminary graduate, yet because of his effectiveness he was asked to teach church planting at the Manila-based School of Theology.

Can an 18-year-old boy plant a church in the midst of Polish immigrants who are strong Roman Catholics? Yes, with the Lord's help I was able to assist in the birth of the Pioneer Baptist Church in Pioneer, Missouri. The Lord called me to preach the Gospel when I was working with the FBI in Kansas City. No one has ever been more shy than I was. I could not speak before a group of people. But the Lord strongly impressed upon me that I was to preach the Gospel. After a time of resistance, I gave in. But before I surrendered to preach, the Lord had already laid a small community upon my heart, a community without an evangelical church. I was to go there to help begin a new church. It was during those days I learned that with God anything is possible.

I am not saying it is easy or normal for a young woman or a young man to plant a church. In most parts of the world there is the age factor that makes it difficult for a young person to relate to and command the attention of older people. But I am convinced white-haired men and women will listen to anyone who has a powerful anointing of God, an anointing that is strongly evident in their walk and talk.

Missionaries appointed to positions such as school teachers, business managers, treasurers, dorm parents, theological educators, medical doctors, agriculturists, and on we could go, can and should be directly involved in planting churches.

One missionary said to me, "How can I plant a church? I am not a preacher." This may reveal how far we have drifted from a Biblical and practical concept of ministry. While I was lecturing in a major American seminary, an attorney asked me, "If, with God's help, a person like me can plant churches, why does our mission board require that we get degrees to equip us to be preachers, when we never have had a sense of calling to be a pastor in the US or anywhere else? And why does our sending agency require that one have so much practical pastoral experience before being qualified to go to a foreign land to plant churches, when I do not feel called to preach or be a pastor?" These were good questions that should be answered.

A seminary degree rarely will give practical assistance to anyone to equip them to plant churches, especially in a foreign land. A businessman without a college or seminary degree may be just as effective in planting a church as a person with a Ph.D. from a college or seminary. As a matter of fact, the called and committed businessman may sometimes be more effective since he cannot rely on his own wisdom and ingenuity. His only means is the Word and the Holy Spirit. The essentials of effective church planting are still the Word of God, the Holy Spirit, the Sower, and the Soil. This is not to say a Ph.D. cannot be effective in planting churches; it is saying the high scholastic attainment is not the essential ingredient. If sending agencies want to make serious impact upon the world's masses, they must realize "laymen" need not be trained to be United States pastors in order to be used mightily as full-time church planters. If sending agencies feel the planter is to become the pastor of the church he plants, it is something altogether different. But normally in a foreign culture, the planter should plant the church and assume the pastor will be a national. Yes, a person going to a mission field in any capacity should have the opportunity to be involved in planting churches. You do not have to "preach" to start churches.

To change directions will call for a radical overhauling of much of the current theology and expectations, not only at the mission board levels but at the grass roots—in our churches. Generally, "laymen" are not expected to do much and consequently most meet that expectation.

Many more church members could be keys in church planting if they were taught and turned loose. Farmers can plant churches. Business people can plant churches. Professionals can plant churches. It is not always a full-time job to plant one church. It can be done as a sideline. There is a need to dehumanize the concept of the role of church planting and make it a God-centered venture open to more people. This means the success rests in God's power rather than in man's ability or training. This is not to minimize man's part or the need for preparation; it is to maximize the place of God in the venture. "Laywomen" and "laymen" played a significant role in the unhindered expansion of the Gospel through the birth of churches in the New Testament.

Chapter 4

Our concept of who

What Are We Seeking to Plant?

It is important to have a clear understanding at this point. A planter's concept of what a church is will make all the difference in the methods used in planting the church. His concept of what a church is will strongly influence his idea of who can plant a church. If church is synonymous with a large organization and programs, not so many people can plant churches. If church means there must be a certain kind of meeting place with a steeple on top, not many can plant churches. If a church means a special building of any kind, not many can plant churches.

In church planting which is unlimited and unhindered, we must understand that the local church is an organism brought about by the Holy Spirit long before it needs to have buildings, extensive programs, choirs, etc. In church planting we should start at the beginning and allow the church to develop its own programs as needs are realized. In its own time the church will meet the needs of having a permanent meeting place, and this will progress as the church needs space for worship and education.

We must answer clearly what a church is before we can think of objectives and strategies.

I believe a perverted and tarnished view of what a church is constitutes one of the greatest hurdles faced by church planters. Unless a Biblical view of the church is clear, the road of church planting will be rough and uncertain. Sometimes preachers leave successful pastorates in the United States and go to a foreign field to plant churches, only to realize that, in spite of a seminary degree, there must be a complete reorientation on the simple question of what a church is. In the States they may have always thought of the church and all the trappings, many of which are very good, as being essential for a church. A study of the New Testament, out of the context of our tradition, may bring us to a fresh understanding of what a church is. One of the problems we will become aware of is the gap between the theoretical and the functional. Now to the question.

What Is a Church?

Jesus Christ said, *I will build my church, and not even death will ever be able to overcome it.* Matthew 16:18 Perhaps the greatest picture of the church is seen in the book of Ephesians. Paul describes the church as the living and powerful body of Christ.

A church has an organizational structure, but a church is much more than an organization.

A church cannot be brought to life by man or sustained by man, only by Christ.

A church is not only godly in its origin, but also in its future and purpose.

A church may meet in a place made by human hands, but the church is much more than the building where meetings are held.

When we speak of a church, it should be recognized that we are talking about the New Testament concept of church. What is the New Testament concept?

The Church as the Body of Christ
(Based on Paul's Letter to the Ephesians)

1. The church is related to God's eternal plan. *of the ages*

God has an eternal plan for the universe and for all people. From Ephesians we read about God's plan and purpose.

Even before the world was made, God had already chosen us to be his through our union with Christ, so that we would be holy and without fault before him. Because of his love God had already decided that through Jesus Christ he would make us his sons—this was his pleasure and purpose. . . . In all his wisdom and insight God did what he had purposed, and made known to us the secret plan he had already decided to complete by means of Christ. This plan, which God will complete when the time is right, is to bring all creation together, everything in heaven and on earth, with Christ as head. All things are done according to God's plan and decision; and God chose us to be his own people in union with Christ because of his own purpose, based on what he had decided from the very beginning. Let us, then, who were the first to hope in Christ, praise God's glory! Ephesians 1:4-5, 8-12

Also in Ephesians 3:9-11 we read, *God, who is the Creator of all things, kept his secret hidden through all the past ages, in order that at the present time,* **by means of the church**, *the angelic rulers and powers in the heavenly world might learn of his wisdom in all its different forms. God did this according to his eternal purpose, which he achieved through Christ Jesus our Lord.*

The idea of the church is not new; it is older than man's earthly history. It is a part of God's eternal plan for creation. Note in the above verses the words **eternal, plan, purpose,** and **by**

means of the church. The church is eternally relevant; it is essential in God's purpose. God knows where history is going. He knows where nations are going. He knows the beginning and the ending of man on earth. The church is a vital part of His plan for creation.

2. Christ is the head of the Church.

Listen to the words of the Bible, *Christ rules there above all heavenly rulers, authorities, powers, and lords; he has a title superior to all titles of authority in this world and in the next. God put all things under Christ's feet and gave him to the church as supreme Lord over all things. The church is Christ's body, the completion of him who himself completes all things everywhere.* Ephesians 1:21-23 Also in Colossians 1:18 the Bible says, *He is the head of his body, the church; he is the source of the body's life.*

Christ is the originator, the designer, the architect of the church.

3. Christ is the source of the church's:

◆ Pardon
Please take time to read Ephesians 2:1-10. Verse 1 says, *In the past you were spiritually dead because of your disobedience and sins.* Verse 4 says, *But God's mercy is so abundant . . .*

◆ Peace
For Christ himself has brought us peace. Ephesians 2:14

◆ Power
And how very great is his power at work in us who believe. This power working in us is the same as the mighty strength which he used when he raised Christ from death and seated him at his right side in the heavenly world. Ephesians 1:19-20

4. The church is one body with many working parts.

◆ One Body
Paul speaks of one body and the unity of that body, *Do your best to preserve the unity which the Spirit gives by means of the peace that binds you together. There is one body and one Spirit, just as there is one hope to which God has called you.* Ephesians 4:3-4

Paul encourages the believers to preserve the unity. Just before he tells the believers to preserve the unity, he gives the secret of how this can be done. In Ephesians 4:2 he says this can be done when believers are humble, gentle, and patient.

◆ Many working parts
Paul tells of this in Ephesians 4:7,16: *Each one of us has received a special gift in proportion to what Christ has given. Under his control all the different parts of the body fit together, and the whole body is held together by every joint with which it is provided. So when each separate part works as it should, the whole body grows and builds itself up through love.*

5. Every member of the church has a special work to do as a part of the total life of the Church.

Concerning the church, Paul says, *So when each separate part works as it should, the whole body grows and builds itself up through love.* Ephesians 4:16

What is a church?

It is the fulfillment of the work of Christ—the body of Christ. Peter majestically describes the nature and mission of this unique spiritual family. *But you are the chosen race, the King's priests, the holy nation, God's own people, chosen to proclaim the wonderful acts of God, who called you out of darkness into his own marvelous light.* I Peter 2:9

The Local Church
(As seen in the Acts of the Apostles)

Ephesians gives a telescopic view from above history telling how all believers relate to Christ and the Kingdom of God. Acts gives a close-up microscopic view of a local (one geographical area) group of believers who are a part of the body of Christ. The book of Acts, as well as other books of the New Testament, gives primary attention to the local church, the church in action.

The same five truths regarding the church as the body of Christ also apply to the local church.

A local, New Testament-principled church is **related to eternity**. It is a part of God's plan for the universe. It is a group of believers who are commissioned to participate in the expansion of God's Kingdom through sharing their faith with unbelievers.

A local church recognizes **Christ as the head** of the group.

A local church understands that **Christ is the only source** of pardon, peace and power.

A local church experiences **oneness** or **unity** within the membership even though there is a **variety** of gifts.

A local church knows that **all parts** of the body, every member, **must function**, must do his part if the entire membership is to grow.

From a study of the first chapters of the Book of Acts we see that a **local church is:**

A group of people who have turned from their sins to place full trust in Jesus as Savior and Lord. They are then baptized by immersion. These individuals continue to meet on a regular basis as members of the family of God. They will fellowship in prayer, praise, and Bible study for the definite purpose of glorifying Christ and expanding His kingdom on earth. This is a church.

This group called a church is more than a social organization. It is special because:

1. The Holy Spirit of God brought the group together.

The members of the group are "**called out ones**" with a special purpose. (A New Testament Greek word used to describe those who made up the early church is **ekklesia,** which means called-out ones.)

2. There is a special, supernaturally-produced union among the members.

Koinonia is the Greek word that describes this union, this special relationship between believers. It is Christian **fellowship**.

3. There is a common commitment.

In Acts 1 we find the secret of the power of the early church. All the members were committed to:

- **The Living Lord** (Acts 1:3) There was no doubt among the believers that Christ was resurrected and that he was alive.

- **The presence and power of the Holy Spirit** (Acts 1:4-5)
They received God's promised gift—the Holy Spirit.

- **The second coming of Jesus (Acts 1:10-11)**

These three great truths formed the doctrinal foundation for the early church. They are evident throughout the book of Acts. The believers acted as they did because, without a doubt, they believed these three truths. They shared a common ideology, a common philosophy about the place of God's people in the development of history. Life was more than existence, more than making a living, more than having an earthly family; it was being a part of God's eternal family.

4. **There was a common commission.**

They had a reason for living and even dying if necessary. Acts 1:8 tells us of that mission in life. *But when the Holy Spirit comes upon you, you will be filled with power, and you will be witnesses for me in Jerusalem, in all of Judea and Samaria and to the ends of the earth.*

The sharing of the Living Lord in the power of the Holy Spirit became their reason for living. This was their mission in life. All they did was related to this mission. They met to share. They met to pray. They met to study. They met to fellowship. All of their meetings and organization were related to an effective sharing of the Good News of the living Lord. The bold proclamation of the Good News was always an outgrowth of times of prayer and fellowship. Organizational structure was developed when necessary to enhance the life of the church. The church was able to spread quickly because the members were busy sharing the faith rather than trying to keep the organizations running smoothly.

The church of the New Testament was like light in darkness. Wherever members went, they took the light of the Gospel and dispelled the darkness. Into the homes the loving church went; into pagan religions the church went; into courts of kings the church went; to the poor the church went, always changing the hearts of people through the power of the proclaimed Word.

A local church of today is to be nothing less than the New Testament church as described above. **A church is** a band of believers filled with the Holy Spirit, set out on a mission to lead people from darkness to light. The church penetrates society with personal love as she uses her sword, the powerful and holy Word of God. This church will be victorious. Every church must always give attention to the basics of prayer, fellowship, and feasting on the Word. These are the fountains of life for the church.

If the great cities of the world are ever significantly touched with the Gospel, there must be a fresh concept of the permeating church. There must be the knowledge that a church can thrive, even without a meeting place it owns. As long as the church can be confined within four walls, it will not greatly affect society. The danger today is thinking of the church as an organization that controls the lives of people rather than people, an organism controlling the organization for objectives greater than itself. Many groups are busy building organizational structures and edifices to the neglect of the organism. In builders' language, this is constructing scaffolding and seeking to develop a superstructure before proper concentration on the foundation. The secret is the organism which can be birthed only by God.

What is a church? It is a group of people, born of God, filled by the Holy Spirit, who come together because it is natural for a family to come together to take care of the Father's business. The Holy Spirit produces groupness. The family shares a

Christian world view they come to understand and cherish to the point of living or dying for that purpose.

I have wondered why the Communist movement in the Philippines has thrived as it has. It is a rather recent movement, yet in such a short time the communists were able to grasp the total allegiance of so many. Some people left their families to go to the hills or underground, risking their lives. For years newspaper headlines and features related to the threat of the "insurgency," yet when you drove the streets of Manila or in the provinces, there were no signs of these people. There were no Communist bookstores, no Communist headquarters on any main street. On the other hand, we see so many signs indicating the presence of various religious groups. We have our book stores, printing presses, schools, hospitals. But seldom do we make front pages as ones who are revolutionaries. What is the difference? We know Communism is a deadly ideology and Christianity is a living hope. The difference may be in an understanding and a commitment to a world view that makes enough sense for a person to give his life to it. If the average church member is asked why he is living, you will seldom get an answer much different than from an unbeliever. Part of the positive answer to the problem is thinking through the New Testament view of the church, how it fits into God's plan of the universe, and the relationship of each member to that plan.

Sometimes church and denominational leaders wax eloquently about the harvest and all the plans to reach the harvest, yet seemingly are oblivious to the fatal sickness abounding within associations, state conventions, and mission boards called turfism and programitis which dwarfs dreams and drains resources. As long as the church is bound in our current theological box, we are blowing air without substance. Any church that can be contained by a building is not a new Testament Church.

Furthermore any group which is controlled by an organization lacks the freedom to be what it is purposed to be and do.

As church planters, dare we think in such a way that spells sure failure? Rather, we must think of the church as a living organism, empowered to be salt and light to change and preserve. It is to be seen as permeating, penetrating, and changing by its presence, a presence that includes the carnate witness as well as the incarnate witness. It is fluid in that it can flow through condominiums, high rises, and hard-to-get-to places. Organizational structure can be used and is needed by a church, but the organism should only develop organizational structures when, and as long as, they enhance the well-being of the organism. In the beginning of church planting, the attention must be on the birth of the organism. Out of felt and real needs, the necessary programs and organizations can be added. The foundation is laid first, then the superstructure is built. We must beware of losing focus and becoming professional scaffolding builders. It is one thing to plant a church where the family of believers (the organism) becomes one, inhabited by the Spirit; it is something quite different if the church planter seeks to develop the programs and organizations first. It is like the builder who tries to develop the top story of the building at the same time he is developing the foundation. Few can do this, and anyone who tries faces insurmountable odds to effectively planting an indigenous church.

If one has in mind that the church to be planted must immediately have the organizations seen in a 20-year-old church, the approach to planting will be different than if he is thinking of the birth of an organism as seen in the New Testament. What is included in the whole picture? What are we attempting to plant? If it is a full grown, fully developed church with all the trappings that come through years of development, it will not be easy and will take years.

After about five hours of lecture in one seminar, the participants kept questioning how a church could be planted in such a short time. They could not imagine a self-governing, self-supporting, and self-propagating church being planted in six to twelve months. I was not only saying this is possible in responsive areas, but the cost would not necessarily exceed a few dollars. I finally realized that we were talking about two different things, two different concepts and views of a church.

For many the word "church" brings to mind the building and all the things inside. In due time all of these may be a part of the church life. But one does not begin there in the planting stage. When we think of the basic definition of a New Testament church, what must we have in order to have a genuine church?

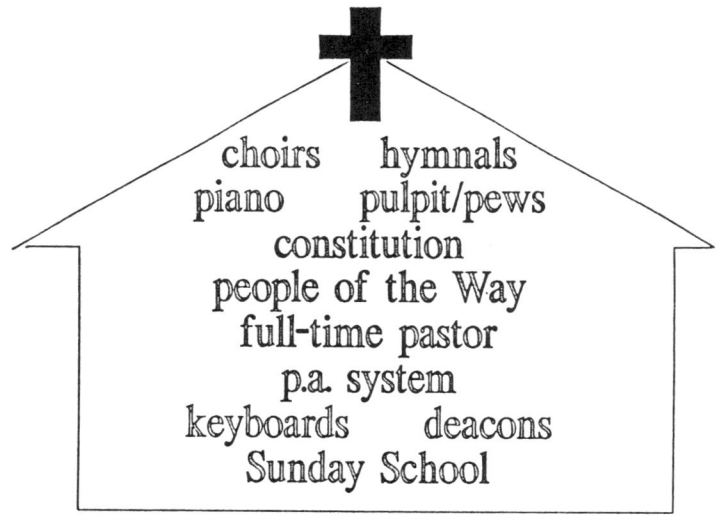

Can we have a church without a choir? Yes, we can. Can we have a church without hymnals and a piano? Yes, we can. What if from the above picture we erase pulpit/pews? Yes, we can have a church without them. What if we erase constitution, full-time pastor, p.a. system, keyboards, deacons, and Sunday

School? Can we have a real church without all these? Yes, we can. Even without a church building, can we still have a real church? Yes, without a doubt.

Of all the things in the sketch, what must one have in order to have a church? **People, people of God, people of the Way, people who are unique because they have Christ living within.** It is here that church planting begins. Please note again the definition of church given previously in bold print.

This is what a church planter plants.

As the church develops and is able to provide them, many things may be added, but this is primarily the responsibility of the church.

Chapter 5

Roles of Ministry For the Pastor and Church Members

How do the pastor and the members fit into God's plan for the church? God does have an eternal plan for mankind which can be understood by His people. The Bible clearly reveals what God has done in the past, gives us a picture of some of what He is doing now, and gives us a glimpse of what He will do in the future.

We know that in the past mankind fell into sin and was separated from God. In an effort to draw man back to Himself, God used great men who related to Him by faith. Then he chose the Jewish nation and worked through it to demonstrate His love. God sent prophets to speak for Him. Last of all God came to earth Himself in the person of his Son, Jesus. (John 1:14) Jesus preached repentance and forgiveness, and men killed Him. In His death Jesus became the sacrifice, the payment to set sinful men free—if they would, by faith, accept the sacrifice. Once a person accepts Christ as his Savior and Lord, he becomes a co-laborer with Christ, part of God's team destined to change the world. The Bible says, *Those whom God had already chosen he also set apart to become like his Son, so that the Son would be the first among many brothers. And so those whom God set apart, he called; and those he called, he put right with himself, and he shared his glory with them.* Romans 8:29-30

Jesus spoke of the life of His followers when He said, *"Believe in the light, then, while you have it, so that you will be the people of light."* John 12:36

Christ established the church to be responsible for sharing the Good News. In Ephesians 3:9-11 Paul speaks of the eternal plan of God and the place of the church. *God, who is the Creator of all things, kept his secret hidden through all the past ages, in order that at the present time, by means of the church, the angelic rulers and powers in the heavenly world might learn of his wisdom in all its different forms. God did this according to his eternal purpose, which he achieved through Christ Jesus our Lord.* For more insight about God's plan for the universe, read Ephesians 1:9-12.

The church is to be victorious. Jesus said, *"I will build my church, and not even death will ever be able to overcome it."* Matthew 16:18

The Biblical church is made up of those who have been born again and have followed Christ in baptism. In the New Testament these are known as people of the Way. They are called believers. God has a clear plan of conquest for these people.

In Ephesians Paul speaks about the various gifts that God has given to His people—each church member. Every gift is to be used in building up the body, the church. The church is built up as it grows in spiritual maturity and as it adds new members.

This is the expansion of God's Kingdom on earth today. While in its earthly stage, the church will never be the dominant force, but its influence will be felt, and it will become a threat to the forces of evil all over the earth. Christ is the head of the church and the source of its life; the church is not weak and insignificant.

Now back to the idea of various gifts given to members. These gifts are to be used in the expansion of God's Kingdom. The Bible says, *It was he who **gave gifts to mankind**; he appointed some to be apostles, others to be prophets, others to be evangelists, others to be pastors and teachers. He did this to prepare all God's people for the work of Christian service, in order to build up the body of Christ.* Ephesians 4:11-12

He gave various gifts of ministry. These gifts were meant to be used to build up the body of Christ. **What is the role of the pastor and the members in the development of the local church?** What is the work of the pastor and what is the work of the church members in the expansion of the Kingdom of God?

We will look at two common views of ministry. First, the popular **traditional view** and second, the revolutionary **Biblical view**.

The traditional view became popular when the Christian religion was spreading throughout the Roman empire and caught the attention of Emperor Constantine. Constantine realized it would be a good political move to join forces with this rapidly spreading religion. So he declared the pagan Roman empire to be Christian. The church was diluted as paganism identified with

Christianity. This was the beginning of a thousand years of dark ages for the church. The Bible became a book for the educated clergy only. The common man was at the mercy of the clergy who told him what to believe. The church leaders were not to be questioned. Many of the religious leaders were not Christian in nature. The Roman church became more corrupt as it was led by corrupt religious leaders. A concept of ministry was being molded which is still prevalent, even in Protestant and evangelical churches. Ministry was for the professionals. The members simply followed. Power was in the hands of the clergy.

The Great Reformation of the 16th century brought some change as Martin Luther declared the Bible should be open to the common man and that anyone could pray directly to God. But much of the "Dark Age mentality" hangs on in the minds of religious leaders today. There is a need for an extension of the Reformation so that, not only will man be able to enjoy the privilege of direct access to God, but also will accept the corresponding responsibility to minister.

The gap between the clergy and laity is still too great. God's people need to be set free to minister in meaningful ways in the world as well as in the church. Many people are bored with a religion "attached" to their lives. Only when work and religion become related can God's eternal purpose have meaning. And only as a person is consciously a part of God's eternal plan will life be filled with direction and joy.

The **traditional view of ministry** may be better understood with the following illustration.

Traditional View of Ministry

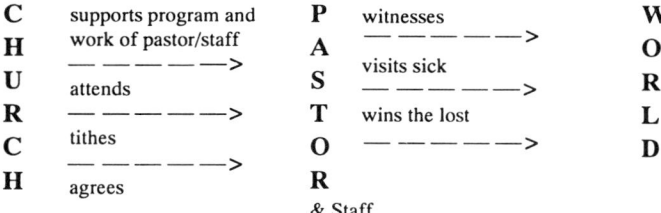

In this traditional concept of ministry, members are called "laity."

The work of the laity is to support the pastor as he does the ministry.

This support comes in three forms:
- Attend
- Tithe
- Agree

If a member does all of these he is a great member.

A layman is someone who is not trained or skilled. So he cannot be trusted with too much of the real ministry. He supports the pastor and the pastor's program.

In this concept of ministry, the "laymen" tend to be lazy, and rarely will they win someone to Christ. Usually the best they can do is take someone to The Minister.

The pastor is recognized as the professional minister.

He is called "Father," "Reverend," or "Pastor."

He is considered as The Minister.

When the layman finds someone who wants to be born again, he must go to The Minister to get help and direction.

Usually in this system, the pastor dominates the worship service, since he views the members as "only laymen."

The ego trip can be great for the pastor. He enjoys the titles and limelight.

The pastor is the only one at the front lines of battle in the world.

The pastor usually is not taken seriously by the world. He is "paid to do this," the people say.

The world is not won to Christ, and the pastor wears himself out in trying to do all the ministry.

Some pastors and members have grown tired of these roles of ministry and have gone to the New Testament seeking a more meaningful concept that will liberate the clergy and the laity.

Next we will look at the Biblical concept of ministry.

Biblical View of Ministry

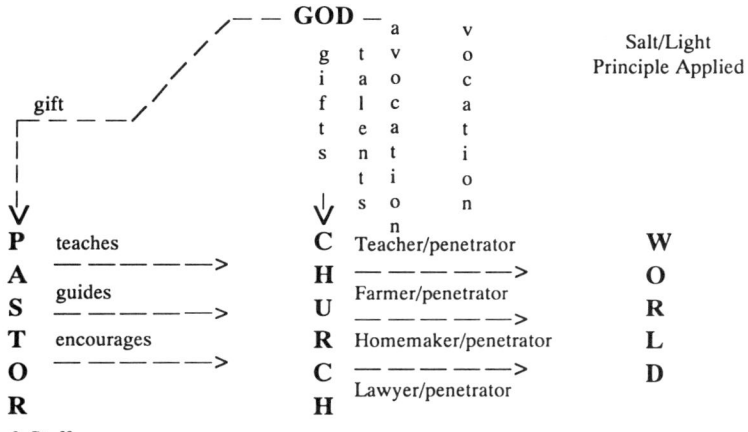

The pastor is the equipper. His primary work is to equip the members so they can minister in the world.	The members are trained, therefore not laymen. A new believer is a layman, but if he remains a layman for more than six months, the pastor and church should re-evaluate the programs of the church.	The world is where the members live.
He is a minister, not The Minister.		When sharing their faith, they are not seen as paid salesmen; they are known as satisfied customers.
A pastor must be out among the members so he can know the needs of the church body. This will enable him to properly feed them so they will be equipped to minister effectively.	A church with 100 members should expect to have 100 ministers (not pastors).	They are full-time ministers where they live and work.
	Members now find meaning to life in their church and work, properly relating their church/work life to God's eternal plan.	All levels of society are being penetrated.
The pastor is the player/coach. His work is more meaningful now that he is an equipper.	Their vocation is the same — world penetration, using their God-given talents as a means to reach the world for Christ.	
The pastor must be in the world doing various ministries, but his primary ministry is equipping the body.	God gives gifts to the members to minister to each other. These gifts include teaching, encouragement, sharing, prayer, and others, as the body needs.	

The pastor ministers to ministers so they can minister.

Chapter 6

The Lifestyle of the Church Planter

The lifestyle of the church planter is an inevitable topic to be faced on most mission fields. This often is a critical issue when missionaries from advanced, industrialized nations are working in third-world nations. The sending bodies expect their missionaries to live on a level somewhat comparable to that of their native land. The physical and mental well-being of the missionary should be respected. Missionaries find it natural to continue living on a level similar to the one they are accustomed to if it is possible. This may be a level above many of the people in underdeveloped nations. There are those who live in such a luxurious fashion that it is right that the national Christians complain about it. There should be a happy medium that will not hinder the ministry of the church planter.

It is not in the best of taste for a missionary to seek to live like a king in any land. But it may be just as detrimental for one to intentionally make himself live like a pauper. In being accepted, the inner heart and attitudes are more important than the lifestyle. If an average American went to Manila to plant churches, he would be expected to be himself. He is seen as an American, therefore is expected by Filipinos to live on an American economic level. For the planter to consciously and conspicuously cease to be an American would be artificial. If his heart is right with God and filled with love for the Filipino people, he will be able to minister effectively and maintain his own identity. If he decides to "acculturate" fully as one in a lower economic level, he may choose to sell his car, move into a house without screens, and eat rice three times a day. What will the people think about him? They will think he is crazy and a person of poor judgment. For him to give up what everyone strives for doesn't make sense. He becomes artificial and condescending.

When thinking of becoming "acculturated," the tendency is to forget that in many places such as Manila and other cities in third-world countries, there are masses of people who are not poor and homeless. The giant city of Manila is jammed with automobiles, most as nice as the ones driven by missionaries, and many much nicer. There are multitudes who live on the level of the average pastor in the United States. I have worked in affluent subdivisions where, for economic reasons, I could never consider renting or buying. These, too, are Filipinos with whom we must be able to identify. Southeast Asian countries are filled with the latest electronic inventions and gadgets. Many of such items have either been brought in from America, Japan, or other nations or are being produced in the local economy.

Acculturation should not automatically be thought of as doing without or living on a low economic level. There are those who say one must become fully un-Americanized. It is not wrong to be a healthy American. It is not something to be ashamed of.

But what about Jesus? Didn't He empty Himself? For sure He did, but you can count on this: He never forgot who He was and where He came from and who His Father was. He did not sever ties with His Homeland and Father. As a matter of fact, I have a hunch He was longing to go back to the Father. He came to a foreign and different land; He adapted. He lived within the culture, but He kept in touch with His Heavenly base and Father.

There are extremes which must be avoided. One extreme is seeking to over-identify. To seek to become fully one with the strange culture is not normal. Several years ago an anthropologist from the University of the Philippines spoke at our annual church planters' conference. He told about the missionary in the far northern part of Luzon who felt he must fully identify if he was to be effective. He removed his western clothing, put on a g-string and proceeded to be one of the people. They thought he had lost his mind. He was forced to leave the country. This is a foolish extreme that brings loss of respect. People expect us to be who and what we are and love them as they are, where they are.

To adopt an extreme posture in seeking to identify is not always healthy, either physically or spiritually. What about seeking to fully identify oneself with the culture when it is contradictory to the Bible? For example, lack of discipline is one of the greatest problems. If the extremist must fully identify, he will cease to be disciplined and his children will not be disciplined. In many cultures, children are not disciplined the way the Bible says they should be, such as the oft repeated message of Proverbs stating if you never discipline a child, you do not love him. What about the church planter who must fully identify and adopt the thought patterns of a nation that fails to discipline and control the children? On and on we could go to the point of the absurd, even to a very non-Christian lifestyle. The only lifestyle the planter must be fully committed to is the lifestyle of Jesus Christ, and that applies primarily to His spiritual lifestyle. It does not mean that we are to wear His kind of clothes or have His hairstyle or wash feet every time we enter a home. The greater the identification with His essential person, the more effective the church planter will be.

Does this mean we are to be indifferent to the new culture and people around us? Of course not. We must strive to identify and understand the culture. The "ugly American" has no place in Christian ministry anywhere in the world.

There is the other extreme which must be avoided, the living-it-up lifestyle. There is a common sense that ought to be a part of the planter. If he lives in the most plush houses and has a chauffeured Mercedes Benz, he is removing himself from ministering to many people. But if he is ministering only to the wealthy, a lifestyle that matches theirs may not be a detriment to ministry. The message of Christianity is not that one must be poor and destitute in order to minister effectively.

One of the most effective church planters I know is a Filipino who lives in a beautiful marble house and has a chauffeur-driven Mercedes Benz. His ministry is to Filipinos of all classes, but primarily his church planting is among the lower, lower-middle class. How would it affect his church planting if he announced that he was going to move into a nipa hut and trade his Mercedes for a bicycle? It would be disastrous. People would pity him and lose respect for him for making such a foolish decision. Doors would be closed to many of the poor and certainly to the more wealthy. It is not what one has, it is what he does with it. What is in the heart makes all the difference. This same wealthy Filipino has started a church among the poor people living a short distance from his house. He relates well because he loves them. His house is open to them. He conducts a special Bible study/leadership training once a week in his house. The people come and feel at home.

A person can artificially bring himself down to the physical level of the poor, yet not be able to minister to them unless his heart is genuine. It is well to remember that physical poverty is not synonymous with piety.

The foreign missionary must remember his children when he is thinking of proper identification. If the missionary could fully de-Americanize his children, is he doing anyone a favor except fulfilling his perverted ego, an ego that can be fulfilled only by successfully grafting on a new culture to the point that the old is obliterated? He may be able to cope, but what about the children? They may do very well until they go back to their homeland they have been taught to forget. They still will have a spark of the American in them, but they don't fit into the culture. They are torn between the two cultures, one of which they left behind in that foreign land. They do not really belong anywhere. This will leave them very vulnerable to drift with others who feel they don't belong. Because of this, many missionary kids (MKs) feel more at home in the company of foreigners who have come to the United States or with minority ethnic groups. They may feel more at home in the company of social misfits who are drifting outside the culturally accepted norms. This adjustment is further complicated for the MK back in the United States when he encounters the obvious lack of commitment among nominal evangelicals. This lack of commitment is in such sharp contrast to the commitment among new believers in cultures where it is unpopular and often costly to follow Christ. This leaves MKs disappointed and sometimes disillusioned.

It is often a difficult adjustment for even the best prepared MK. Why, in the name of ministry, should parents make it tougher? While the children must be allowed to remain Americans, the parents have the responsibility to teach them to abolish unhealthy nationalistic walls. It is not unusual for children to grow up resenting a foreign culture when it is lacking in basic discipline and morals. Some way the MK must be taught to respect and love every nationality in spite of cultural differences. There should be an atmosphere where the children can interact with national children and grow to love them, establishing deep friendships. Children should not be fully isolated from nor overly protected from the foreign culture.

How is the church planter family able to prepare the children for reentry into their native culture at college level? First, the values of the Christian home must be a part of the child growing up. The child must know that dad and mom will not sell him down the river in the name of Christian service, even church planting. The saying is true, "There is no success that compensates for failure in the home." The saddest words ever to come from an MK's lips are, "My parents never had time for me; they were always doing 'God's work.'" The Bible says the man (even a missionary) who does not properly care for his family is worse than an unbeliever.

Second, the child's values and allegiance to his home country must be taught and reinforced. It is right to remember the holidays of his homeland with special celebrations. To know the history of his homeland should be a normal part of his education. To appreciate and respect the distinct culture of his homeland is healthy. A healthy attitude and pride in his nationality should be instilled in the child.

For the church planter, lifestyle is important; it can be a curse or it can be a blessing. His health, physical, mental and spiritual, will be affected by his approach to lifestyle. It makes a difference to his family and certainly to those to whom he desires to minister. Some find themselves leaving the field of service prematurely because of not being able to cope in a different culture. Nothing helps more than the security of knowing where one comes from, where one is going—all in Christ—to be a participant in the victory march with God in Kingdom expansion though the birth of church after church.

Chapter 7

The Church Planter and the Language

Nothing will capture the attention of a group of unbelievers like the foreigner speaking clearly in their native tongue. Paul was able to communicate when he used the native tongue of his hearers. In Acts 22:1-2 we see the power of a commonly understood language. *"Brothers and Fathers, listen to me as I make my defense before you!" When they heard him speaking to them in Hebrew, they became even quieter;* . . . Speaking the language of the people is of primary importance in effective church planting.

There are two areas of concern the church planter must hurdle if he is to be a strong indigenous church planter. One is finding a handle with which he can feel comfortable and aggressive. The other is learning to communicate in the local dialect or language. Failure at either of these points leaves the planter vulnerable to the temptation to leave church planting and move into social ministries or other kinds of missionary work. There is nothing wrong with social ministries or support ministries, but they may not be the same as New Testament Pauline church planting. There are those who never learn the language yet stay in church planting, but must always speak through someone else. This severely limits church planting and takes away much of the joy. There is nothing more exciting than being under the control of the Holy Spirit and feeling the message flow freely, a message in the tongue of the hearers.

A big part of the miracle of Pentecost had to do with language. A multitude was present, people from various nations. It was essential that they understand the message of God, so God performed a linguistic miracle. The Bible says, *All of us hear them speaking in our own languages about the great things that God has done!* Acts 2:11

For many, learning a new language is not far from a miracle. There is stress no matter what the language program is. There is, in a real sense, taking on a new culture as one learns a new language. Language and culture are so intertwined that to have one means sharing in the other to some degree. A living, daily use of a new language means giving up some of the old culture and accepting a new and different culture. There will be physiological and psychological strain in learning the new language.

The strain is enough that full concentration must be given to learning the language. This means that, even in the presence of a burning desire to get into church planting, months must be set aside solely for language learning. This will not be easy for the man who has come out of a successful pastorate in USA fast lanes. His style and tempo of life changes drastically.

The same is true for the mother whose primary responsibility has been a Christian homemaker and co-laborer with her husband. Care must be taken not to abandon the children at any time to learn the language. There may be no other time so difficult to maintain a Christian home where every member is attended to properly than in full-time language study. There is no better way to make a loving mother fighting mad than for an insensitive language director to imply that learning the language is more important than the well-being of her children.

The church planter must pay the price of learning the language because of the needs of the hearers. The deep needs of the hearers can most adequately be met when they hear about sin and the Savior in their own native tongue. It is the heart that must be reached. The people's native tongue is their heart language, the language of their will and emotions. When they are confronted with something so intimate as the life-changing Gospel of Jesus Christ, they need to hear it in their heart language. In this way the message can penetrate every part of their understanding and being.

The church planter must learn the language if he is to accelerate church planting through reproducing churches. If a person does not hear the Gospel message in his native language, he is not only limited in his own understanding; he is seriously limited in being able to share the message with others. I have heard of the experiences of Filipinos who had come to Manila from other provinces where other dialects were spoken. They were converted and trained in a language such as English or Tagalog. When they returned to their homes to share their newly found faith, they found it is very difficult. They had not learned the way of new life using their own dialects. On one occasion, a young woman, a seminary graduate, was asked to share at an association meeting. The language of the meeting was Ilocano, her native dialect. She refused, saying it would take such a long time to prepare something in her dialect. She had been trained in English, using Western English thought patterns and language. She spoke in Ilocano in ordinary life, but when it came to spiritual matters, she had little to say. Another told me that she could not even pray in her native dialect when she went back home because she did not receive the Good News of Christ in her native tongue. If the people use their native dialect in normal living and revert to a foreign language to convey spiritual truths, these truths come across as foreign and unnatural. When God calls out leaders from among the new believers, it is a serious hindrance to their ministries if they must receive their training in a foreign language. (There are exceptions to this when English is almost an equally used second language.)

A simple rule: if new believers are not able to communicate the Gospel message effectively in a second language such as English, their leadership training should be in their native language.

There is no better way to communicate love than to speak to people in a language they can understand. Nationals feel good when they see the foreigner sweating over learning their language. They sense that he must really love them. If the language is learned early, more churches will be planted later.

Every church planter can learn a new language if he is motivated properly. Language programs may serve as avenues to help and enhance language learning, but the key is personal motivation. If the planter wants to badly enough, he will learn the language. The motive for the church planter is no less than a personal commission from God to communicate a lifesaving message to spiritually dead people. The love of God, the love for God, and the love for lost people will be the driving forces in language learning.

Chapter 8

Concentration: This One Thing I Do

Paul's narrow-mindedness of purpose contributed to his success. He set his eyes on a life-consuming adventure and never let anything distract him from it. His words ring with purpose and a single-minded commitment. He said, . . . *the one thing I do, however, is to forget what is behind me and do my best to reach what is ahead. So I run straight toward the goal in order to win the prize,* . . . Philippians 3:13-14 In I Corinthians 9:25-26 we read, *Every athlete in training submits to strict discipline, in order to be crowned with a wreath that will not last; but we do it for one that will last forever. That is why I run straight for the finish line;* . . .

Why are church planting missionaries tempted to be sidetracked from giving full time to church planting?

1. Lack of a clear, indisputable call to New Testament missions will leave the planter vulnerable to filling up his time with other good things.

2. It is easy to become sidetracked when the language is not learned.

3. Failure to get hold of a church-planting "handle" which is easily understood and usable will open the door to good activities which are not church planting.

The church planter of today must be determined to run straight for the finish line, to keep his objective of planting churches foremost. There are things which may distract—things which are very good, yet are not church planting. Let's look at a few of these.

1. Moving into ministries that are primarily social.

One can give out rice without speaking the language, having a handle, or feeling a call, yet have a feeling of satisfaction. Since this is a delicate area for many, let me say that this is not a put-down or judgment on anyone involved in social ministries. All of us should, to some extent, be involved in social ministries, but social ministry is not always the same as church planting.

Knowing the local language is not as essential to carrying out social ministries as it is to conveying deep spiritual truths. Conveying spiritual truths requires verbal communication. We all know about the incarnate witness, the life of service and love. However, an atheist can give his life (a demonstration of love) for the social betterment of others and never touch the deepest needs of man. The planter must seek to live like Christ, but he must also convey a carnate message about the life, death, burial, and resurrection of Christ if his is to be a distinctly Christian witness. The planter who does not get the language will face a greater temptation to get involved personally and exclusively in social ministries because this may be his only option. He will find it difficult to do otherwise if he cannot speak deep spiritual truths in the local language. One need not have a church planting "handle" to engage in many social improvement activities.

No one denies the overwhelming physical needs abounding in the world today—needs for better diets, better sanitary conditions, better livelihood opportunities, etc. Paul no doubt saw poor living conditions in his day; yet he realized that the best way to help people raise their living standards was through expansion of the Kingdom through the multiplication of churches. More long-term social assistance is given through the planting of Christ-centered churches than any other way. When the head of a family is born again, his life will be changed. His priorities change. His vices begin to disappear, leaving more money for basic family needs. His work ethic changes; he becomes honest and reliable, and consequently new job opportunities open. The local church, through its program of teaching and training, has the responsibility to meet social needs. But seeking to meet social needs without first helping people to have a new heart will bring short-lived changes. The more a church planter gets involved in social improvement programs, the less time he will give to church planting. I have faced the temptation to set up local co-ops and small self-help programs from poultry and rabbitry to piggery and gardening. But I felt that to get involved would hinder my goals in church planting. Those things would be good and are needed, but as a church planter I must ask myself the question, "Is this New Testament church planting?" No doubt there is a sense of satisfaction that can come from such social programs. There will be those who say church planting can be done better as one is giving his time to helping people physically. For some this has been a successful way to plant churches. But if a person can follow Paul's example and go to the heart of the problem, why not do it?

2. Involvement with bureaucratic maintenance.

Fortunate is the church planter who is stationed far away from the missionary concentration. To live in the area where the institutions are located, the headquarters area, makes the church planter too accessible to serve on committees of the mission. There is a need for boards and committees, but the temptation to serve can sometimes be too great for the church planter. Some enjoy being on committees, being in the know about all mission business. Some think it is a mark of importance and a little ego boost to be invited to oil the machinery. I am not suggesting that church planters never serve on committees; I am saying too much time given to this good thing can take away from concentrating on church planting. A church planter can destroy his career as a church planter by being on too many committees and boards. It is commendable if a mission will allow a new church planter to be fully free to plant churches at least his first term on the field.

3. Becoming an advisor, director, or coordinator of existing work.

If a planter goes to an area where a fellowship or association of churches already exists, the leaders may expect him to become their advisor or at least their "on call" man at all times for supply preaching, baptizing, performing wedding ceremonies, dedicating babies, etc. A missionary can become so involved in doing what the nationals should be doing that he ceases to be a church planter. This can become a tremendous ego trip for an American in a third-world nation. He can become an authority figure like he never could have dreamed possible in his own home country. Add a bit of money to throw around and he can become next to God in the eyes of the people.

What is a church planter to do if he is assigned to an area where there is the temptation to become less than a church planter? First, he should have fixed firmly in his own mind what his job is. If he is not sure how to plant churches, the temptation will be greater to follow a role that is not really church planting, or he may rationalize by saying that he is a "catalyst." Second, he should let the people know his objectives. It does not mean he is going to be less than a brother in the Lord and co-laborer; it does mean that he is not going to be a "baby-sitter." His job is to plant churches which hopefully will join in fellowshipping with the existing churches. The planter will be a prayer partner, a co-worker in sharing dreams and strategies. He will be an encourager. He may become involved in leadership training, but nothing should replace church planting.

Every church planter should develop a healthy relationship among the existing churches in his area. He can plant churches in harmony with them, but if he senses a call, has a "handle," and speaks the language, he can personally model church planting. He can work hand in hand with others and when it is necessary, he can go it alone. In pioneer areas where there are no churches, he may need to plant some without the presence of any other Christian leaders. Without the language or a "handle," there may be the need for "companionship," someone to interpret and do what the planter cannot do. Knowing the language and having a "handle" will add boldness and confidence necessary for a person to go into an unevangelized area and win people to Christ, then lead them into a church family relationship.

4. The danger of looking back.

Church planting will suffer when the planter's attention is divided between the here-and-now church planting and the place, people, and days in his homeland. There are two distinct times when this temptation is strongest.

◆ **The beginning, the arrival**

After arriving on a foreign field, facing a new culture, learning a new language, it is not unusual to think of the good old days at home. Parents, brothers and sisters, uncles and aunts take on a new meaning, they are missed. The days get long when you are like a child, facing language learning and adjusting to a new way of living. Not all nations move at the pace of the American. There may come the fleeting thought of "What's the use? Let's go back." Proper orientation will help in these days of adjustment. But it is the call of God which brought the planter to the field, and that call becomes even more important to keep him there. An obsession with the past can hinder church planting.

- **The time when children go home for college**

This time calls for a deeper commitment and a reevaluation of the call of God. To see the kids one by one return to their homeland to go it on their own is not easy and should not be expected to be so. It is at this time that many consider seriously going back home at least for a few years. The stress of separation can take its toll on church planting. It can divide the attention to the point that church planting becomes secondary.

It is not abnormal to have the above times of stress. It is expected that the Christ-controlled planter can cope through the strength that Christ gives. Strength comes from remembering the things of God are more important than all the conveniences and security of living in a known culture. Added strength comes when we remember God loves our family and children so much more than we ever could and that He will care for them.

Looking back too much was costly for the Israelites. It can also be costly for the church planter.

5. The church planter can be diverted by materialism.

You may be saying, "Can this be true of a person who has committed himself to church planting?" It happens often to pastors and evangelists in the States. Why could it not happen to a foreign or home missionary? It does happen. Sometimes things and money take enough of the planter's time and attention that it diverts him from doing his best in church planting.

Failure to learn the language and get hold of a "handle" will leave the door open for the planter to retreat into existism. He will find it more comfortable and safer working on the car, running errands, etc., doing things that "need" to be done just to live. Just keeping western gadgets operative in a third-world setting can border on materialism. Anyone who has lived in such situations will attest to the fact that basic existence does take a lot more time than it does in the States. The pace is slower, the lines are longer, the red tape is unending. Instantaneous everything is not available, which means canned and frozen foods are not available; drinking water may have to be boiled; milk has to be mixed up; rice must be cleaned before cooking; to say nothing of keeping appliances working. This can be frustrating, but it is a way of life, and the quicker the missionary accepts it, the better. This can steal so much time that the missionary must be careful lest he become a maintenance man just existing rather than one who ministers that others may live eternally.

The church planter may be as preoccupied with the stock market reports as the pastor in the US. When there is no monitoring, a missionary may grow wealthy. This can happen when a missionary is supported by a number of churches and individuals in the States and one does not know how many others are providing support or how much each is giving. It would be very difficult for each supporter to travel halfway around the earth to check up on the way money is being used. The fellow with good contacts and personal charisma can be tempted to build an empire. The missionary working under a board has an advantage in that the salary is fixed and is based on faith in the generosity of supporting churches. He does not have to solicit; rather he can concentrate on getting the job done.

Escape exits are always available to the person who does not learn the language, has no clear sense of calling, or who cannot or will not find a handle. Three things will keep a planter on track:

1. The clear call of God.
2. The ability to use the language of the people.
3. Finding a "handle" that is Biblical, user friendly, and effective.

SECTION II

FOCUS BEFORE STARTING

Chapter 9

Know Your Parameters and Determine Your Objectives Before Starting

The person who does not know his objectives walks with the certainty of a blind person. Someone has said, "If you don't know where you are going, any road will get you there." What would you think of a builder who decides to build a house without a plan or idea of what he wants to build? He goes down to the lumber company and says he wants lumber and materials to build a house. He says, "I am not sure what I need; just give me a lot of everything." A good builder knows what he is going to build before he begins. He knows what materials will be used and how to use them. Should less be expected of a church planter?

Knowing clearly our objectives will help us in defining the absolute essentials. We must know our objectives if our strategies are to be meaningful.

The objectives will determine the strategies and methodologies. A fuzzy objective will result in uncertain steps and techniques. The objectives must be clearly delineated before beginning down the church-planting trail.

Through the years my objectives have been threefold:

1. The salvation of individuals;
2. The birth of New Testament-principled churches;
3. The birth of an indigenous association of New Testament-principled churches.

Later when we deal with the very practical aspects of church planting, we will look in greater detail at the objectives.

A church planter should master one technique and then be flexible as different occasions arise. There is no doubt there are many ways to reach the same objectives, but there are some parameters within which all must stay if New Testament churches are born. What are the fixed parameters? They are quite broad and general.

The Book: The Bible

There is only one Book worthy of our proclamation—the Bible. One planter may bring people to Christ through lessons based on one book of the Bible, such as John. Another may preach a series of sermons from different portions of the Bible. Another may use Biblical stories of certain men and their relationship with God. Others may use the chronological storying method, moving from Genesis to Revelation. But there is one thing in common, it is the Book. The more we let the Word speak, the purer God's message will be to the masses. There is the temptation to enhance, and preach we must, but there is nothing like the Word of God. Occasionally we need to be reminded that *our* word, even when teaching and preaching, is not the Word of God and does not carry the same power.

The Man: Jesus Christ

The primary secret for success is not a method, nor is it the planter. The key to success is not in a set of doctrines nor a style of worship. All of these are important and may be instruments used by God. The Alpha and the Omega in the cosmos, as well as in church planting, is Jesus Christ. He is the One who makes the difference in the unbeliever. He is the head of and source of strength for the new body of believers called a church.

He will not share His glory with anyone else. To try to permit a human personality to share His rightful position cannot be in Biblical church planting.

The Agent of Change: Holy Spirit

The messenger takes the Good News of Jesus Christ in the enlightening, convicting, and converting power of the Holy Spirit. It is He who is in control, never to call attention to Himself or bring glory to Himself; rather He is in it all to lift up, magnify and glorify God's Son, Jesus. In John 16:14, Jesus speaking of the Holy Spirit said, *He will give me glory.*

The People

God builds churches with people, not wood or stone. People without Christ are the reasons for church planting and expansion, all to the glory of God, now and forever.

A **messenger** of God, under the direction of the empowering **Holy Spirit,** taking the **Word** that reveals the **Man** to the **masses,** are the parameters. To move within these parameters as the Holy Spirit leads takes the mechanical and monotonous predictability out of church planting. It is dynamic, never static. There are boundaries and guidelines, but they are wide enough to allow the effective functioning of all God's people with their various personalities and gifts.

Chapter 10

What is an Indigenous Church?

The word "indigenous" means something native, domestic, national. It is that which springs from and develops within a particular culture. Farming with a carabao is an indigenous method of farming in the Philippines. An indigenous church is a contextualized church. It is able to grow within the culture where it finds itself, without outside interference or control. The indigenous church planting/church growth pattern, under the leadership of the Holy Spirit, sets people free to be and do what God intends. Indigenous church planting is sowing the Gospel seed in the native context of thought and things, allowing the Holy Spirit to do His work in His own time and way.

Missiologists often use the term "self" in describing an indigenous church. For fear that the oft used "self" leaves a feeling of too much of self in the accomplishment of something, the term "Christ-sustained ability" may be more Biblically accurate. 2 Corinthians 3:4-6a states it well: *We say this because we have confidence in God through Christ. There is nothing in us that allows us to claim that we are capable of doing this work. The capacity we have comes from God; it is He who made us capable . . .* In all of the "selfs," the centrality of and the dependence upon the indwelling Christ must be uppermost in our minds if the new church is able to be indigenous in its practice.

This great truth of a Christ-sustained self-reliance is beautifully portrayed in Deuteronomy. Moses said, *"The commandment that I am giving you today is not too difficult or beyond your reach. It is not up in the sky. You do not have to ask, 'Who will go up and bring it down for us, so that we can hear it and obey it?' Nor is it on the other side of the ocean. You do not have to ask, 'Who will go across the ocean and bring it to us, so that we may hear it and obey it?' No, it is here with you. You know it and can quote it, so now obey it."* Deuteronomy 30:11-14

There are at least **five "selfs"** in the indigenous church.

1. The indigenous church is **self-governing.**

From Colossians 1:17-18 we read: *Christ existed before all things, and in union with him all things have their proper place. He is the head of his body, the church; he is the source of the body's life.*

Also in Colossians 2:19 the Bible says: *Under Christ's control the whole body is nourished and held together by its joints and ligaments, and it grows as God wants it to grow.*

Self-governing means the local church is able to make its own decisions under the Lordship of Jesus Christ. The local church should never be under the control of any foreign body. A foreign body may be a fellowship of churches such as an association or convention. The local church may voluntarily cooperate with such groups of churches, but a group outside the local church should not assume authority over the local church. The church should be able to think and act on its own. This can be especially difficult in third-world nations when well-intentioned missionaries, especially foreigners, bring their ideas and pre-packaged programs to a church or an association of churches and ask the people to consider adopting them. As one key Filipino leader asked, "How can we Filipinos say no to an American missionary?" He went on to say, "We may not agree on the proposals, but we are conditioned to say yes."

From the beginning the local church should have the freedom to decide when they will meet, where they will meet, and what they will do when they meet. The local church should, from the birth of the church, be expected to decide who the pastor/leaders will be, how they will be paid, etc. The local church should decide where and when to build their new chapel. The local church should decide when and how they will have evangelistic crusades.

The church may listen to the missionary, but should not allow the outsider to make decisions for it or put it in a position where it cannot say no to suggestions that do not fit its needs.

2. The indigenous church is also **self-supporting.**

Read again the verses from the Bible given under the first point, self-governing. They apply here also.

Self-supporting means the local church takes care of its financial needs through the tithes and offerings of its members. From the beginning of the life of the church, this is possible. It must be remembered that a new church will not have the financial responsibilities of an older church. As the church develops a step at a time, it will also grow in its capacity to finance its programs and needs as they develop. Third-world nations have become so accustomed to dependence on foreign help that for a church to think self-support is revolutionary. With God's help it is being done by many churches. These churches have a healthy spirit of who they are and what they can do with God's help. Those who simply say, "We cannot," are to be pitied. Those who would say this may have never really tried.

The danger of dependence on outsiders is seen in Hosea 7:8-11, *The Lord says, "The people of Israel are like a half-baked loaf of bread. They rely on the nations around them and do not realize that this reliance on foreigners has robbed them of their strength. Their days are numbered, but they don't even know it. The arrogance of the people of Israel cries out against them.*

In spite of everything that has happened, they have not returned to me, the Lord their God. Israel flits around like a silly pigeon; first her people call on Egypt for help, and then they run to Assyria!"

Self-support begins very early in the life of the church. Before the church is born the people provide the meeting place, the lights, and the chairs. After the church is born, the members continue to provide the meeting place, the song books, Bibles, etc. In the beginning the church usually does not need a church building. This becomes a long-term project of the group. They will begin to save money for land and building. In the beginning a church may not need, nor can it afford, to import a pastor from another place or from a seminary. The church will recognize that God can call and empower members from within the church to lead the worship services and perform the duties of a pastor. The church will pay the expenses for the leaders to attend training seminars and classes which usually will be made available. As the church and leaders develop, one man may be chosen to be the pastor, with others helping him. As this pastor gives more and more time to the work of the church, the church will want to begin giving him a set amount of love offering each week. As the church grows, it is possible a full-time pastor will be needed, and the church will pay him a salary on the level of others in the community.

When the church has an evangelistic crusade there is no thought of asking someone else to help finance it.

The self-supporting church has a dignity unknown to beggars.

3. The indigenous church is **self-teaching.**

Paul said to the church in Rome, *My brothers: I myself feel sure that you are full of goodness, that you have all knowledge, and that you are able to teach one another.* Romans 15:14 Again in I Corinthians 14:26, 31 Paul says, *This is what I mean, my brothers. When you meet for worship, one person has a hymn, another a teaching, another a revelation from God, another a message in strange tongues, and still another the explanation of what is said. . . . All of you may proclaim God's message, one by one, so that everyone will learn and be encouraged.* The building up of a healthy local church is greatly dependent on a participating membership wherein every member uses his God-given gift to help build up the entire body. (I Corinthians 12 and 14)

Teaching is being done when a church involves members in public Bible reading. To young Timothy, Paul said, *Until I come, give your time and effort to the public reading of the Scriptures. . .* I Timothy 4:13

One of the greatest examples of self-teaching I have experienced is seeing a church having a Bible reading report time. Every member was expected to read a minimum number of chapters weekly and report to the church. (For further study of this simple program of Bible study, note Chapter 24 which deals more fully with this topic.)

4. An indigenous church is **self-expressing.**

Our tendency is to assume every church should express itself in worship the way we feel comfortable with and accustomed to. It is likely the planter will greatly affect much of what goes on after the church is born. Somehow he must be big enough to allow the new church to have its own personality and ways of expression.

As long as Biblical doctrines and principles are not violated, any cultural expression is acceptable. Culture influences worship expression. There is no problem in allowing the culture to be seen in worship.

Some churches will want to meet more frequently than others. The planter need not tell the new church they should have prayer meeting at 7:00 on Wednesday night, Sunday School at 9:45 a.m., and worship at 11:00 a.m. I will never forget one new church started in the northern part of the Philippines. Immediately after their baptism and the birth of the church, they began coming together early Sunday mornings for worship. They might have some singing and a sharing time, Bible study, and then more music and prayer. They did not know about the time of Bible study with an intermission for those who wanted to smoke or go home. All morning they worshipped. Every night they came to the little chapel to share and pray, discussing their experiences of the day. Should I have introduced "prayer meeting" to them? They expressed themselves as they felt right, and it was beautiful.

5. The indigenous church is **self-propagating**.

In Matthew 28:18-20 Jesus said: *"I have been given all authority in heaven and on earth. Go, then, to all peoples everywhere and make them my disciples: baptize them in the name of the Father, the Son, and the Holy Spirit, and teach them to obey everything I have commanded you. And I will be with you always, to the end of the age."*

Self-propagating means the church will be involved in starting other new churches. It is normal that a church filled with hope and joy will want to share their new faith with as many people as possible.

Self-governing and self-support come at the very beginning of the life of the new church. Self-propagating does not come as quickly. It takes time for a church to bring about the birth of another church, but from the very beginning there should be a "heartbeat" for starting another new church. It may be as simple as a church member going to a nearby town or barrio and having a Bible study at the house of a friend or relative. Once there are new believers who are willing to follow the Lord wherever He leads, a new church can be born. A church should not rest until it is involved in spreading the Gospel in such a way that a new church is born.

In starting new churches, God can use farmers, homemakers, professionals, businessmen, students, anyone fully committed to Him. A person does not have to have Bible school or seminary training in order to start a new church. The indigenous church should be able to start another new church in the same way it was started.

An indigenous church established upon Biblical principles and fully yielded to Christ is a vibrant, living, and exciting body of believers, confident and courageous in spreading the Gospel. Some of the chief characteristics will be the "selfs."

Chapter 11

Identify Your Target Before Firing

At some time a church planter will have to deal with the subject of targets. Who am I going to try to reach? Sometimes missions and missionaries spend a disproportionate amount of time trying to determine the proper target, but a serious church planter will have to include this in his thinking. At one time our mission organization became very preoccupied with targets. In meeting after meeting, in large and small groups, this was the topic of discussion. It dawned on me one day that we could spend hours talking about who we should target and leave the meeting, walking past multitudes of people without thinking seriously about their lost condition. Not knowing which target to shoot for is not our problem. Our problem is being motivated enough to aim for the obvious, nearby targets—those within our sight, our voice, our touch, yet never touched with the Gospel because we are worn out from discussing who to target.

Some say to go after the rich so they can provide support for future work. This line of thinking includes financial support as well as leadership. I have not personally met any missionary who thinks like this who is effective in any kind of church planting. Part of the fallacy is the idea that if the rich are reached, they will have a great influence on society at their level and downward. Seldom will the rich be able or willing to reach the poor people. Another fallacy is the idea that the rich will be more effective in changing history. Great movements in history—revolutions which have made a difference—did not come from a movement among the rich. If we want to change society and the course of history, we must be aware of that sector of society which has within it the greatest capacity to think and effect revolution. The rich and elite are not the ones; they have it made and would rather things not change. They do not want their status and security threatened. They like history; it has dealt them a good life. These people also tend to be fixed in their way, their web of friends and lifestyle. Arrogance and pride are common to this class. They have the answers and do not need help. These are the reasons they are so closed to the Gospel. Does this mean that we are never to target them in church planting? Of course, we should never ignore them; but we must realize that human nature has not changed from the days of Christ. Unless our motivation goes beyond reaching them for what they can do for us, we will be void of the Spirit of Christ who is the secret of our success. They need to be reached because they are lost and God loves them.

What about targeting the very poor in church planting? As is true with targeting only the rich, we must be aware of the leadership of the Holy Spirit and go where He directs. To target the very poor and forget and ignore the middle and upper classes may be just as calloused as targeting only the rich.

Some people feel more at ease working with poorer people and are therefore more effective in working with them. God may lead a person to concentrate his work among poorer people, but no one with Christ in him can be blind to the spiritual poverty of any sector of a Christless society.

Which socio-economic group will have the greatest potential of changing history? The poorest of society are not the ones. Often the poor are too deep in a fatalistic rut to dream dreams. They are not able to see the prospects of revolutions which will change history. They see themselves as lacking education and opportunities. They tend to give up, just living out life as they find it. Discipline is not usually a strong characteristic of the very poor. Disciplined people change history. This does not mean we should ignore the slums and squatters. If they are not born again, they are doomed just as anyone else without Christ.

Who has the greatest potential for changing the course of history? What class of people are most apt to make a difference in a nation? It is the lower-middle and middle class. These tend to dream dreams of what they can become and do. These, not being rich, have little to lose and much to gain. They live at a level of flux. They are out of the cellar of poverty, yet do not feel they have all the answers or all out of life that they want. Generally, it is this sector which is most responsive to the Gospel. They have not only the capacity to be visionaries, they have the necessary discipline to pursue dreams.

Many church planters tend to spend more time with this level of society, just as Jesus and His disciples did. This is the level I have found best to concentrate on, without eliminating the other levels as potential targets for church planting. I feel very comfortable having a church planting Bible study with the rich on one night, the middle class on another night, and slum dwellers on another night, hoping to plant churches among each.

Some people are able to reach one level of society more effectively than others. It is difficult to imagine Christ deciding that He will concentrate on only one level of society and ignore the others. The Lord may lead one person to concentrate on the rich and someone else to concentrate on the poor, but neither can forget nor ignore the masses in various levels of society. I believe it is best to move at the leading of the Holy Spirit, without predetermined boundaries.

Chapter 12

Finding a Place to Plant a Church

Every situation is different and every church planter has a different personality. There is no one way which is always best for finding a place to plant a church. But there are some things I can share which have worked for me, some of which are common for many.

1. There must be a burning desire to plant churches.

A person who is only casually interested will not find as many open doors and opportunities as the one who is "eating and sleeping" church planting.

2. The successful church planter must know what he is looking for.

He must know the kind of place he is looking for and the kind of response he is looking for. He will be aware of advantages and disadvantages of certain locations. He should be sensitive to anticipations of people who open their homes or businesses to a Bible study or worship service.

3. The planter must know what it is he is seeking to plant.

If he is hoping to start with a full-grown-church-type worship service from the beginning, he will be looking for something quite different than the person who is thinking of starting with a smaller group of unbelievers. For those whose interest is instantaneous-big-church, it will be almost necessary to steal a lot of straying, disgruntled sheep, often from smaller community churches where first-class facilities or leadership are not available. The planter who has this as his goal will be looking for outside financial support before he can look seriously for a place because he must have "high visibility." We are not going to deal with finding a place for this approach since it will not likely result in an indigenous church. Rather, we will be thinking of the natural, reproducible way which is not dependent on the presence of foreign capital or control. There have been many churches started from small groups which grew naturally into much larger groups, and as they grew they provided personnel and financial support themselves. There is nothing wrong with a small church becoming a large church, as long as koinonia prospers and the mission of the church is carried out by the members.

◆ Finding a Place to Plant a Church in Pioneering Areas

We will assume the Lord has put you in a specific place for the primary purpose of starting churches in that area. Your place of abode very likely will relate to getting started.

Common sense and Biblical examples tell us that surveying is a part of conquest. In Joshua 18:3-10 we see the value of mapping out an area. *So Joshua said to the people of Israel, "How long are you going to wait before you go in and take the land that the Lord, the God of your ancestors, has given you? Let me have three men from each tribe. I will send them out over the whole country to map out the territory that they would like to have as their possession."* Note some key instructions for this survey ordered by Joshua: *"Write down a description of these seven divisions and bring it to me. . . ." So the men went all over the land and set down in writing how they divided it into seven parts, making a list of the towns.*

The experience of Nehemiah is a classic example of a person doing a survey of an area before deciding how to move forward. In Nehemiah 2:11,13 we read, *I went to Jerusalem, and for three days I did not tell anyone what God had inspired me to do for Jerusalem. Then in the middle of the night I got up and went out, taking a few of my companions with me. . . . As I went, I inspected the broken walls of the city and the gates that had been destroyed by fire.*

It is rewarding to read the first chapter of Nehemiah to see what must precede a survey. We see a broken heart, a confession and cleansing of sin, and then a vessel ready to go survey the area of need.

STAGE I: General Survey

Government agencies are generally happy to supply all the information you need about the demographics of an area. Some agencies which may help you are those dealing with planning, statistics, mapping, development, etc. Often, these people are glad someone is interested in learning more about what the government is doing. Maps and statistics may be available free of charge or for only a nominal fee. From the study of these materials you can begin to get a feel of the area. You will want to know the political boundaries, state or provincial boundaries, populated areas, colleges and universities, etc.

The next step may be called the **windshield survey.** Whether in a motor vehicle or not, it is necessary to get out and move about the general area. As you go, you are thinking and praying church planting. You will begin in the area where you live and gradually move on to outlying areas. If you live in a large city, there may not be an immediate need to do much surveying far away from the city. (I don't feel that we must limit the leadership of the Holy Spirit to the city in which we live, even though this may be our starting point.)

Below is a list of some things you will look for as you make a general survey.

1. Natural boundaries, such as major highways, rivers, and mountains
2. Major population centers
3. Industry, trade, commerce, farming
4. Economic levels of the people (Note the extent of the gap in the living conditions between various levels.)
5. Ethnic groups, size, and language
6. Dominant religions in the area (You will note the presence of houses of worship, taking into account the number of those which would be classified as evangelical. By the presence of religious facilities you may learn what religious groups are targeting that area. The presence of a church building does not always mean the community is being reached by that group.)
7. Areas where there are no religious facilities

STAGE II: A specific area or community

Knowing the particular area to target demands a lot of prayer and work. I am convinced the Lord has contacts who are waiting for our coming. It may be a person, it may be a family or small group. It may be a small group of believers who have transferred to an area and do not know what to do about starting a new church. For sure, the Lord will open the doors as we go. Seldom will the contact be made if we sit in our office and wait.

Approaches will vary from country to country. In a country where the predominant religion is not Christian, the approach may be quite different. Not having experienced this, I cannot speak with any authority. In some countries, it will be more difficult to find people who are open to even being friends with anyone of a strange religion. But in all countries, a survey will be helpful. Being among the people and developing friendships will be essential. Where little or no seed has been planted, the planter must begin where he is relationally with the people. It may take time and circumstances to build relationships through which the Gospel witness will be shared. But we must remember we are not dealing with a lifeless and powerless Gospel.

When you are sure the Lord is speaking to you about a certain area, your work is not over; it is just beginning. After you have located an area you feel is the right place, it is necessary to search more thoroughly for those whom God has prepared, those who are open.

◆ Finding a Place to Plant a Church in an Area Where Churches Already Exist

The planter must be aware of pockets of people in areas where there are no churches and begin praying for those areas. He may be able to locate one or more families who have transferred to the area and are open to becoming the core group for the new church.

· Through surveys and contacts

Working with a local church is often preferred. Various church planting strategists would give it different names, but the following are some common ways to work with the local church in church planting.

• Through church family members

First, the local church must be led to church growth sensitivity and commitment. After this has been accomplished, gather all the members together. Display before the group a large map of the general area, pointing out the population centers, developments, and trends. Locate any other evangelical churches on the map and mark the location of the members with colored pins. Draw a circle around the immediate community being ministered to by the church and note the church members living beyond that circle. Take note of the presence of several families living in a community which is a distance away from the church building. Begin to look closer at the total population of that community and note if there is an absence of adequate worship centers.

A closer study may be needed at this point. The presence of an evangelical church does not necessarily mean that the church is reaching the community.

After recognizing there is a need for added outreach in the community, the next question is, will these few families from the local church be willing to form a core to begin a new church? Will the pastor and leaders be unselfish? If they are determined to permit only home Bible studies or cell groups which must remain under their control and be counted as a part of the statistics for the "mother church," new churches will not likely be born. If the church is willing to give up members so new churches can be born, the bulk of the battle is won.

Note the location of single families living far from the inner circle of ministry. One person or one family is all that is necessary to serve as a contact or host to spearhead the planting of another church.

Note those families who have transferred to another city, province, or state. Perhaps they can be used by the Lord in planting a new church in their area. A New Testament-spirited church will so sensitize members to world evangelization and train them accordingly that such a transferee will automatically think "church planting" when he moves to another place.

• **Through relatives and friends of church members**

Church members will be asked to identify relatives living in underchurched communities. It is not necessary that the contacts be Christian, but they must be open and willing to serve as a base for the community Bible study.

Church members will then share the names and locations of friends who have been cultivated. These may be colleagues at work or social acquaintances.

The bottom line is, any church who wants to can plant churches. Openings and connections are everywhere for the alert church members. Church members can find places to plant churches. It is the natural way of multiplication. Church planters will not always be able to work with or through an existing church, but when possible there are real advantages.

Chapter 13

A Pause For Some Practical Questions

There are some questions the serious church planter must deal with before beginning the planting of a church. We will address some practical questions most often asked in church planting seminars. Many of them are closely linked to finding the place to have the church planting Bible study.

- What are you hoping to plant?
- What is the nature of the Bible study group?
- What are some factors that influence the size of the initial Bible Study group?
- How many people should you hope to reach at the beginning?
- How can you enlarge the Bible study base (participants) in resistant areas?
- Is it a home Bible study or a community Bible study?
- What kind of meeting place do you need?

◆ **What are you hoping to plant?**

You want to plant the kind of church that can be planted by nationals within the membership. This means you do not want to do anything that will be a barrier to reproducibility. Therefore, even if you have the money, you will not be planning to use paid staff and workers to come in. If possible, you will want to meet in a place which will not require rent.

By now you may be asking what kind of church are we going to plant. We will seek to plant a New Testament-principled church which is self-governing, self-supporting, self-teaching, self-expressing and self-propagating. From the beginning, in every thing you do, you will try to avoid doing anything that will move the church away from these five "selfs" and the Biblical concept of a church.

◆ What will be the nature of this new group?

If the Gospel has not saturated the place, the beginning group will be made up of unbelievers. If the place has been saturated by the Gospel, it is doubtful that we should be there as church planters. Anyone who has not been born again should be potential targets. Believers who have not been grouped into a gathered-church life could be proper targets. Active members of other churches where the Gospel is preached and believed should not be targets. To come in with a superior and "high-powered" program and lure members of other congregations is not ethical, much less Christian.

The best and most wholesome way of church planting is winning people to Christ and gathering them into a church family. This may be slower, but it is so rewarding. A major part of the excitement of the church planting journey is the birth of people into the Kingdom.

◆ What are some of the factors beyond the church planter which will influence the size of initial Bible Study Groups?

1. The religions in the area will make a difference.

The responses of a Moslem area and a Catholic area will usually be different. One is more open to the Bible than the other. In a city where there are massive houses of worship and several centers of religious training, you may find the people closed to revolutionary Biblical teachings. However, if you leave the city and move beyond the overpowering presence of that religion, you may find a greater responsiveness. There are some areas where people receive severe threats from the religious leaders if they entertain the idea of looking into another religion. In one area where I did church planting, our neighbors told us if they participated in one of our Bible Studies, their children would be expelled from the local school. It was very difficult to get a sizable group together for Bible study.

2. Political instability and civil unrest will make a difference.

When people are uneasy or afraid, they will be seeking security and peace. When martial law was declared in the Philippines in 1972, the people we were working with became much more open to the Gospel. They were afraid of the future because they faced circumstances they had not experienced before. But after martial law became a normal way of life, the people were much less receptive to the Gospel.

Financial insecurity will open people to new ideas and change. When all is well, people feel no need of anything new and may resist change, but when the threat of insecurity is faced, there is a new openness.

3. A transient population will make a difference.

Generally, the more fixed a community—few leaving and almost no new faces coming in—the less responsive people will be to the Gospel. Architecture and infrastructure may reveal something about the responsiveness of the people to the Gospel. The greater the change in architecture, businesses, industry, and housing developments, the greater the receptivity to the Gospel. When you drive into a town and see that the streets and buildings are the same as they were a hundred years ago, you will expect that people are not used to change in any area of life. Such was the case in the province of Ilocos Sur where we worked for two years with very little response.

On the other hand, Mindanao, the large island in southern Philippines, has been very responsive to the Gospel. For years it has been the frontier land where people migrate, looking for a better life. As they move away from fixed situations and family ties, they become more open to spiritual matters. In a place like this, it is not difficult to get a group of 20-30 adults and teens to attend a Bible Study.

Missionaries are finding that, when working with tribes, the "deep tribal work" is less productive than the work among tribes living on the fringe between their native land and the areas where civilization is moving forward. In the transition toward a new culture, the people are more responsive to the Gospel. "Deep tribal" refers to more than geographical location, it refers to loyalty to native language, dress, food gathering, religion, etc. People on the move geographically and culturally are usually more open to the Gospel than those who are stagnant in lifestyle. It is no surprise to hear that those working with the deep tribal groups are finding less response than those working with tribal groups experiencing change.

People congregated in larger cities tend to be more open to the Gospel because many of them have moved from their homes in the more rural areas. When they are away from family and peer pressures, they become more open to new thinking. Unfortunately, they also become more open to pressures of evil within the city.

The most responsive sector of society is the student population. Having come away from the fixed surroundings of home, they feel free to explore. Students have come into a more intense exercise of learning and exposure to the world; this helps them to be more open to new ideas. They are often more idealistic and are looking for ways to make an impact on the world. This makes them prime targets for the life-changing Gospel.

4. Socio-economic standing makes a difference.

In many nations it is easy to get people of the lower and lower-middle economic class to attend a community Bible study. It is more difficult to bring middle and upper class together in large numbers. Usually, the higher the level of society, the fewer will attend a Bible study. (I am speaking of people who have not been born again, even though they may be loyal to a religion.) The wealthy often live a life unto themselves and may have very little knowledge of who their neighbors are. To expect them to cross that social barrier erected even within the same class is not reasonable, especially if it has to do with a religion that will challenge their choice of priorities and sense of values. It is unlikely that these people will come to a Bible study held in their community. The rich have their circle of friends and their own priorities and are not going to be very open to the intrusion of a new religion. Among this class it may be necessary to think of smaller groups, even a family or two, and then through relational lines gradually reach out to others with the Gospel.

In the metropolitan area of Manila, one-third of the population is made up of squatters. They live in make-shift houses on someone else's land, often government property. It is not difficult to gather a crowd to attend a preaching service or Bible study. A large gathering may not necessarily mean a sincere interest in religious values. Often a large group will attend a Bible study with the hope of distribution of material goods.

◆ **How many should you have in a beginning church planting Bible study group?**

Is the number important? It depends on your goal. If your goal is a person saved, one is enough to have in the study. If your goal is the salvation of a family, a family is enough to have in the study. If your goal is a church, then the broader the base the more likely you will end up with an indigenous church in a shorter period of time. The smaller the number, the longer it will take to plant a strong church that is self-governing, self-supporting, self-expressing, self-teaching, and self-propagating. Normally, the broader the base, the stronger the superstructure will be.

What are some of the problems to be faced when starting with a very small number? Can a church be started if you have only one family in the initial Bible study? Yes, it has been done many times, **but there are some things one may expect if the church is planted with one family.**

1. Slower growth
It is not ideal to have a church with only one family. The growth will be slower than it would be if you started with five or ten families. It would not be normal to have a church born within six months if you begin with one family. (Again, I am thinking of areas where there are no Christians to begin with.) It may take four months to get one family converted and ready to assume responsible church life.

2. A family dynasty
In some cultures, a problem in beginning with one family is the danger of developing a family dynasty. The result may be that the family reaches only their extended family and the group becomes a family church rather than a community church. Others may have a difficult time breaking through to feel a part of the group.

3. A weak foundation
It will be more difficult to build a healthy and large superstructure on a very small foundation.

4. Lack of moral support

In a nation where it is not popular to be a true Christian, new believers need moral support. A very small group of believers may find it difficult to survive the mockery and persecution of unbelieving friends and neighbors.

5. Limited support system

The smaller the initial group, the slower the growth for a longer period of time. The smaller the group, the smaller the pool from which leadership can be drawn, making the burden greater for the few overloaded with various functions of the church life.

6. Limited number of churches planted

Due to an extended length of time to get a good church born, the church planter will be limiting himself in the number of churches he can plant. The smaller the number, the more likely the planter is to fall into the trap of becoming the leader for an unlimited time. If he stays in the one group and serves as leader for one or two years, he will be tying himself up in such a way that he will not plant many churches. Then he also faces the problem of the dependency of the group upon his presence and leadership. In many nations the longer the church planter stays and exerts leadership, the more cautious the new believers will be in trying their hand at leadership. New believers cannot quickly duplicate the style of a highly-trained church planter. It is not always a sign of strength and love when the foreign missionary controls the new church with his leadership and advice. Sometimes it is a sign of insecurity on the part of the missionary. "His church" may become his security blanket and ego trip.

7. Lower visibility

The smaller the group, the lower the ministry visibility of the group; this affects the pace of growth. At a church planting conference a young church planter came up to me after one of the sessions and said now he understood why after nine months the growth toward the birth and development of a church he was planting was so slow. He spent a long time with one family and then tried to add to this family. Of course it will work, but why not start with a broader base if you are working in a responsive enough area to do so? We must remember, however, that responsiveness is a significant factor. It is true that in some nations beginning with one family or a small group is the norm and, as a rule, the most that can be hoped for.

◆ **How can you enlarge the base in resistant areas by using the cluster approach?**

What can be done to extend the initial base when the people are very resistant to the Gospel and will not come together in a large group? When it is nearly impossible to gather several families to engage in regular Bible study, a cluster approach may be desirable. The cluster approach means having a number of small Bible studies in and around the targeted geographical area. This can be effective in large housing compounds or in high-rise dwellings. This approach will demand much time and energy. A team approach can handle the cluster Bible studies very well. If there are several people participating in the church planting project, they can take care of a large number of Bible studies. Each Bible study group may consist of one or two families. If there are six of these small groups, there may be up to twelve or more families involved. If half of these follow Christ, there is an adequate foundation for a viable church which can survive and thrive. Six families committed to Christ make a good foundation for a new church. The cluster approach can be a full-time job if there is only one church planter involved. The more Bible study groups the greater the need of a team approach, meaning more than one planter may need be involved.

Some things to note in the cluster approach

1. **If there is a team, it is of great importance that the team members share a common theology and philosophy.** If one team member minimizes the salvation experience and leads his group into the larger group in the future, it will weaken the entire witness of the new church. To mix saved and unsaved into the foundation of a new church means havoc and turmoil. If one team member cannot distinguish between a church and a church building and the other team members know you can have one without the other, there will be a difference of emphasis and understanding. A common understanding of the roles of ministry in the pew and in the pulpit is very important.

2. **Each team member must understand the objectives of the effort.** The final objective is the gathering of all the small groups into one larger group which will become a church.

3. **Logistics and scheduling require work and planning.** It is not easy to find six to ten places to begin Bible studies simultaneously. It can be done, but a lot of prayer and leg work is necessary. The timing is significant if the small groups progress somewhat in unison in their understanding and accepting Christ. This presalvation stage is important. Only after the group members have received a new nature can we expect them to be willing to come together with strangers. We will expect the clusters to come together after the members of each group have been saved. The new nature and the indwelling Spirit are the drawing and unifying factors.

4. **The celebration is crucial.** We would expect the new believers to be willing to meet others of like nature. This rally or celebration can be held at a central and neutral place. The meeting place can be a school, a restaurant, a community clubhouse, or any neutral place. (By neutral I mean a place where anyone in

the community would feel free to go.) At this time a religious house of worship is not necessary. Often someone in the Bible study groups will know of available places and may help secure the place. It is not usually necessary for the church planter to rent a place. Expect more of the people; they are capable and motivated now that they have a new Father.

5. **This is a workable plan for churches.** A church has the manpower and, if it is a Biblical church, it will have the motivation and necessary resources. As we will see later, very little money is necessary to plant a church if we follow the Biblical pattern. Any church who wants to can use this cluster system to plant another church.

◆ **Is it a home Bible study or a community Bible study?** A church can be born out of a home Bible study and a church can be born out of a community Bible study. As I have said, where it is difficult to get unsaved people to come together, it may be essential to work on family units. But it is important to remember that the community is the target if we want to have a broad representation in the new church. We must understand the difference between the typical home Bible study and the community Bible study. We need to understand the advantages and the disadvantages of each.

The Home Bible Study

The very term "home Bible study" indicates that the study is in a home or residence. The family dwelling has certain limitations which should be recognized. Meeting in a home does not usually lend itself as readily to establishing a broad base upon which a church will be developed. However, it is possible in less responsive areas to reach one family and then use that family to invite and reach neighbors and friends. When people are responsive and it is possible to get a large group together for a weekly Bible study, it is generally better not to meet in a home.

The home is:

Limited in space
Available space determines the maximum number of participants. There are some homes that can accommodate a large number of people. But if the home is small, it will be difficult to have a "community Bible study" there. The number of participants will be limited.

Private
In most cultures people are reluctant to go into the house of a stranger. Also, in a private dwelling, meetings week after week may result in resentment on the part of the homeowner. This is especially true if he is not yet a believer.

After a few weeks the host may grow tired of being tied down to his own house at the same time each week. He is irritated at the realization that he got more than he bargained for. It did not dawn on him that this Bible study thing was going to last so long. This can be a greater problem when one spouse is open to the Gospel and issues the invitation while the other spouse is not interested. As an outsider, the church planter may not always be aware of this. If the wife issues the invitation, it will not be easy for her to back out so she goes ahead with it. After a few weeks resentment begins to build in the husband and the result will be strife between the husband and wife.

Sometimes there may not be a full understanding of all that is involved when the homeowner agrees to host a Bible study. The planter knows it would be better to have a larger group, people from the community. He and the host will invite neighbors to attend. On opening night the unsaved hosts really feel that their privacy has been invaded. The floors are sparkling clean. Everything is in place and beautiful. It is a rainy night and people start coming in. Most of those who attend are friends of the hosts, but a few are not. A woman walks in with three small children trailing her. The hosts watch as little dirty footprints follow each other across the floor. The host family is a disciplined family, but these kids are not. In the middle of the Bible study, a child goes across the room to look at a cherished stereo. He has never seen such a thing. The buttons move in many ways. As the hosts observe, can you imagine how deeply they are concentrating on the Bible lesson? The home is a private place.

Why not have the study in a home of someone who is a Christian already? First, there may not be such an opening in every community. Second, if there is, it is very likely that the Christian will have similar feelings as the non-Christian. For both, the home is a private abode. It is true that it may take longer for the resentment to build if the host is a believer, but after a time the resentment likely will come. A few meetings may not be a problem, but after a while they will begin to interfere with family plans.

Limited in people who will attend
Social factors may discourage some people from attending a Bible study in a home. Some will not attend because of bad relationships. Most everyone has enemies and the very place of the Bible study may prevent some people from attending. The reputation of the host should be taken into account whether the Bible study is in the house, in the carport, or in the yard.

I encountered this problem when searching for a place for a church planting Bible study in a community of about five thousand squatters. I identified myself as a Bible teacher looking for someone who was interested in studying the Bible. I met a woman who wanted a Bible study at her house, a large house facing a busy street. I explained to her that it was to be a community Bible study which would be open to anyone. I am not sure she really understood that it was for the community. Her living room could accommodate twenty people or more. Size was not the problem at this point, but I knew many would not feel free to enter her house. As gently as possible I stressed that the meetings should be in the yard so more people would know about the meetings and feel free to attend. She gave in and the meetings began. We agreed that there would be seven meetings, one hour a week for seven weeks. After a few weeks, it was clear that only her family and a very few friends planned to attend. It was not the broad representation from the community that I knew was necessary for the foundation of a healthy church. I began to visit in the community. One neighbor said, "I will never go to a Bible study there. Last year her son and my son had a fight and my son was killed." Another neighbor said, "No I will never enter her place. It is filled with sexual perverts." The place for the Bible study makes a difference.

What do you do in such a case? I shared with the group my concern that the neighbors were not attending and suggested we begin to move our meetings from house to house. A young man in the group lived nearby. I asked him if it would be permissible to meet in his house the next week so perhaps his family and neighbors would attend. This is not ideal. I prefer the meeting to remain in one place for the time span of the series of studies. But this was a way out of a problem. We moved, some others did attend, and in due time a church was born. They bought a squatter house and converted it into the meeting place. Eventually, many members of that very family were saved and became key members of the church; but if we had continued to meet in their home, outreach to the rest of the community would have been stymied. I am not suggesting that one should not have a **church planting Bible study at the residence or establishment of** someone with a questionable reputation, but it can be a great hindrance.

Advantages of the privacy in the home

First, it is **quieter** and easier to concentrate in a private home than in a semiprivate or public meeting place.

Second, it is a **controlled** situation. There is less potential for disturbances. In an open public place there may be drunks who like to talk. If it is outdoors there may be dogs who like to bark and children who like to play. In a home setting most people would respect the host enough not to make a scene by trying to debate or argue. The host is the key to tranquillity in the Bible study. He, by being who he is, will normally have control.

There are built-in problems, but if the space is adequate, this can be a good place to start a church. I prefer other places which are more public, but I have planted churches beginning in homes. Where basements are a part of the construction, they may take away some of the disadvantages of meeting in a home where the living room is used.

There are times when home Bible studies are of great value.

Churches should have many home Bible studies as an outreach into the community. I know of one church that is very visible in their community because they take seriously reaching their community for Christ. Their primary way of doing this is through a continuous program of home Bible studies. These Bible studies are not designed to become new churches, but are intended to win people to Christ—people who will not come to "church" before they are saved. The church has had as many as twelve of these home Bible studies going at one time. These are "feeder" Bible studies. A group may have one family or even one person involved. Some may have several families, but a large number is not of primary concern; it is a home or a family Bible study. Later we will look at an effective and usable system of every-member-evangelism through home Bible study.

The Community Bible Study

Note some of the characteristics of the community Bible study.

Community denotes a wider participation.
I repeat, this is an ideal which is not always possible in all nations and is more difficult among the rich in any nation. It has prospered, however, throughout South America, Mexico, the Philippines, Africa and many other nations.

I have been involved with church planting community Bible studies with as few as eight to ten and as many as one hundred. The larger the number, the more likely it will become a "crusade approach" with little, if any, participation by the hearers. While this can be effective, I believe the greater the participation on the part of the people, the greater the chance of their learning and understanding. The typical community Bible study with ten to thirty people allows good interaction among members of the group. The important thing is the possibility of a broader base upon which to see a church develop. A number of families are involved in the community Bible study.

Community Bible study suggests spaciousness.
If the community is the target, the meeting place should be more spacious.

◆ **Note some characteristics of a good place for a church planting community Bible study.**

- **It should be a neutral place.**
It should be a place where anyone will feel free to enter. It should be a place free from political or religious identification. My office was in the Baptist Center in Manila. There were large conference rooms available for use if we wanted to conduct a Bible study. I visited in the community and invited people to attend a Bible study at this place. Not only did we have a reputation, but a very visible sign said Baptist Center Publications. I was not surprised that no one came. It was not a neutral place.

- **It should be semi-private.**
The home may be too private. There are some public places which may not be private enough. Semi-private would indicate exposure to the public, yet having a degree of privacy. In one place in Manila I found a family willing to host a Bible study. They had a small community store with a long bench and shelter along the side of the building where people could meet. This gave a little feeling of privacy, yet it was open to the public. The date was set for the Bible study. I went there on the appointed night and everything looked good until a basketball game began in the open area facing the store. At the same time, at another store the community juke box began producing music for the whole area. This was too public. We moved to another place in the community and a church was born.

- **It should be an accessible place.**
To set the meeting place at the outside perimeter of a community may not be wise. A central part of the community would seem to be the best place. If it is among people who have to use public transportation, it is best to establish the meeting place within walking distance of the people. Remember, before they are saved their motivation will be weak.

- **It should be a spacious place.**
The best way to kill a community Bible study or deny it ever getting off the ground is to have the study in too small a place.

A young couple called, asking me to lead a Bible study in their home. They lived in a small apartment in a condominium. The big concrete driveway along side the condominium provided a great place for the study. The large open gate from the street made the place accessible to the public. I explained to the young couple that we wanted to include their neighbors and others from the community in the study. They preferred to have it in their living room which was very small and could seat six or seven, but they went along with me and we had the study at the entrance to their apartment. A light over the door was adequate. The crowds were never as large as I had hoped, but there were enough people to form a core for a new church. Week after week we continued, until one night as we were waiting for the people to come, it began to rain lightly. Without hesitation the couple began to move inside and we continued to wait. The people came to the door, looked in, and left. That was the beginning of the end for this church planting Bible study. From that point the host insisted that we continue to meet inside. It was an adequate place for a home Bible study, but to reach the objective of the birth of a church with a community base, it was not adequate.

◆ **What are some good places for community church planting Bible studies?**

- A community clubhouse
- A community health clinic
- A school building
- An open plaza or park (if there is a semiprivate place)
- A restaurant
- An office

- A place of business in off hours
- Under a tree (if it is not rainy season)
- In a public garage in off hours
- In a carport, if it is visible and open to the public
- In some homes
- Tent
- Day care center
- Hotel
- Store front
- Apartment rented for nursery/day care and is used for church services. Rent is paid by nursery/day care.

Chapter 14

What Strategy and Methods Will I Use?

The planter must deal with this **before** beginning. To know one simple way to plant a church gives great confidence and boldness. After having led church planting seminars in several different countries, and many in the Philippines, I have been surprised at the great number of people in the field of church planting who have not seriously thought through short- and long-term objectives and how to arrive at those objectives. A great deal of frustration can be expected when one does not know where he is going and how to get there. It is possible to have a systemized Biblical approach in church planting. Later I am going to share in detail one simple method that works for me and many others.

Following are some factors of great importance to consider when adopting a basic strategy and methodology.

1. The Bible should be our guide in missiology.

Paul had a strategy. He knew what he wanted to do. He had principles and guidelines. He thought before and as he was doing church planting. His journeys reveal consistencies. His approach was simple and reproducible. One of the greatest compliments that can be paid a church planter is "that reminds me of Paul's way."

2. The strategy and methodology should be simple.

There is no need to be wiser than Paul. His world was complex, yet he deliberately chose to present the message of the death, burial, and resurrection of Christ. He chose to be simple and clear in his approach.

3. The approach should be reproducible.

In an age when perhaps more than four billion people do not know Christ in a personal way, it borders on immorality for a planter to plant a church without considering reproducibility. The birth of new churches is God's way of spreading the Good News to all nations. God does not will that people be born again without becoming a part of a local congregation of believers. As a baby needs the warmth and care of a family, so the newborn believer needs the warmth and care of a Christian family, and this is the church. As the Gospel claims the allegiance of people, so must churches be born. Churches which produce new churches are a necessity in the Kingdom march. If this is true, the church planter must think reproducible in every aspect of planting a church, from the time the first seed is sown to the actual birth of the church, and as it continues to grow.

One of the five major characteristics of an indigenous church is its ability, in Christ's strength, to reproduce itself. A church does not attain this characteristic easily nor by accident. The way a church is born will influence its ability to reproduce itself. The church planter cannot be sure that every church he plants will start other new churches, but he must do everything possible to point the church in that direction. The chances are much greater that a church will reproduce itself if it observes the church planter modeling reproducibility at every stage.

The planter is teaching something either good or bad in every thing he does, not just in everything he teaches. Every action of the planter becomes part of a lesson learned by the church, even before it is born. The planter's relationship to the church can be likened to a parent-child relationship. The child is learning from every action of the parent, even though the parent isn't consciously teaching and the child isn't consciously learning. Sometimes the parent teaches things never intended. The planter needs to remember the need to think and act in a reproducible way if he expects the church to one day do the same.

Many may say this is not important; just get as many churches started as possible and don't worry about the way it is done. That would be fine if there were not so many people to be reached. One man who is able to plant a church so modeled that very few ever could approximate his success is not thinking world evangelization. He is near-sighted. There may be room for unique models which are not reproducible, but if the world is to be reached, it will be by multiplication and not by addition. Reproducibility speaks of multiplication. It is exciting to start churches that thrive and are starting new churches long after the church planter is off the scene. It is like the man who sees hungry people and, instead of giving them fish, teaches them to fish for themselves. It may be easier and bring more self-glory to give the fish, but after he is off the scene, the end result will still be hungry people.

The following areas where reproducibility must be taken into account may prove to be sensitive to some. Remember, the context is reproducibility.

◆ **Reproducibility and the use of material things**

The strategy the church planter uses concerning material things must be tailored to the economy of the local area. It must be possible for the local church, once it is born, to reproduce itself. The planter should not use any material thing which will make it more difficult for the new church to start another new church.

Basic principle: The planter should not use anything which the people cannot provide for themselves.

An abundance of material aids is not essential to starting a new church. When the planter goes to an area loaded down with things that claim his attention and energy, he is sending a message to the yet unborn church that this is the way to do it. If in a third-world nation he must have a special truck to transport his western gadgets to the place where he hopes to plant a church, he may be sending wrong signals as to what is really important. For sure, the people will associate all he uses with the process of planting a church. He may go to an area where there is no electricity. He takes his auto and the special adaptor to create electricity, or he may prefer to take a generator. With this he can have better lights than the people can produce. He can have loud music to attract the people and even show movies. Remember, we are talking about modeling and reproducibility. I am not saying churches cannot be planted using many such material aids, but reproducibility in modeling is important. Without a doubt, the way the planter does it and the things he uses remain in the memory of the hearers, and these things are not reproducible.

Movies attract crowds. Movies have been used in the planting of many churches. I remember going to a community with a population of about 30,000. My desire was to plant a church. I found a place to have a community Bible study. The date and time was set, invitations were given to many people. I went and waited. Finally an old fellow came out and said, "If you will show a film many people will come. Another missionary came and showed a film and more than 300 people came." The first question to come to may mind was, "Where are they now?"

When my family went to the Philippines 20 years ago, I took an accordion. Back in the US I did not know what was involved in mission work overseas. But somehow I got the idea that this thing would help me. After we arrived and saw the place of our assignment and the nature of the work, I knew I had made a mistake. Not only was the accordion not reproducible, I did not even know how to play it. I gave it to a Bible School. It was very likely the only accordion in that province of a half million people. Occasionally one could see a guitar among the people to which we were ministering. That was reproducible, and I encouraged its use.

There are some who think a public address system is essential, no matter where the study is or how small the group. Often this is not needed and not everyone in remote areas has access to such items. (This is not speaking about use of public address systems in crusades, etc., or even by churches that can provide them.)

When the planter is dependent on material aids imported from without, he is teaching lessons which cannot easily be unlearned. When the new church thinks of planting another church, there may be frustration and a tendency to give up if it cannot afford to do it the way the church planter modeled. The material "crutches" used by the missionary appeared to be a blessing, but stymied, stunted, irreproducible growth becomes a tragedy. There is wisdom in being sensitive to the reproductive capabilities of the local economy.

It is healthy to let the people provide all the physical necessities from the beginning. The planter should take himself, the Gospel seed, and little else. Even in remote areas where the people have little of this world's material goods, they are, and should be allowed to be, somebody. They can provide a place, seating, lights, etc., if the planter expects them to.

This is also true in cities. I went out visiting the area near my office. The objective was to find a place to conduct a church planting Bible study. A young man and I went prayerfully to find the responsive person. We walked into a publishing house and asked to speak with the manager. We met her and told her what we wanted. She was the one whom God had prepared. No, she was not a believer, and she had real misgivings about the "born againers." The date and time was set. My friend and I went to her office at the appointed time. She strongly suggested that her employees attend, and she paid them for the extra half hour they spent in the study. Without question she provided the physical facilities.

In the rural area or in the cities, there are people who will provide all the physical things necessary for conducting a Bible study.

In many cultures, hospitality is something the people are proud of. What am I saying to the people if every week I take a load of folding chairs, a lantern, or another lighting system to use in the Bible study? I am saying loud and clear that what they have is not adequate and what I have is better. I would much prefer to go with what the people have than insult them by bringing in something they cannot afford. Sitting on the ground for a Bible study is a great way to go if that is the best the people can provide. I would much prefer having a Bible study with each participant holding an oil light than have it using my imported lantern.

We need to remember that the essentials in church planting anywhere in the world are: The Holy Spirit, The Seed (Bible), the Soil (people), and the Sower (the messenger).

The church planter should give much thought before using imported things. Some are helpful. Some, if used as a crutch or to entertain, are foreign to New Testament church planting. Whatever is used should be within the capability of the local people to provide for themselves. The planter may provide and use these crutches with the idea that later they will be given to the people for their use. But remember this, if the people cannot afford to buy those items, they will not be able to maintain and care for them.

In one province long ago a group of foreign missionaries felt each new church should have a small pump organ. Each church received one. After a period of time, bugs, termites, and usage took their toll and the organs ceased to function properly, even if by chance anyone in the church knew how to play one. Today they are used to gather dust and stack books on. The maintenance was too much of a problem and expense for the local church.

From day one, the church planter should think reproducible. Do not provide any material crutch the people cannot provide for themselves. Is this stingy? No, it is responsible stewardship with the long-term-best in mind for the people.

◆ **The church planter should use a reproducible strategy.**

There are many strategies, some work for some and do not work so well for others. The personality of the planter should be taken into consideration when thinking about the strategy to be used in church planting. But if reproducibility is of great importance, the planter must ask the question, "Is all I am doing in church planting reproducible by the new churches?"

Mass crusades is a strategy used successfully by some. Is it easily reproducible by new churches? In some areas perhaps yes, but in many it would be very difficult. What is involved in having a crusade?

- One must have a good public address system.
- A dynamic speaker is essential.
- It may be necessary to rent a large building.

- Choirs or high-quality musicians must be secured.
- Promotion and publicity will be expensive.
- A well-trained core of counselors must be available.

The list is long. Most newly planted churches will not be able to sponsor such a crusade.

How may crusades be used effectively in church planting? They may serve to soften the soil for future cultivation by the church planter. They may serve to heighten the image of evangelicals in some lands, thus opening future doors for Bible studies. Lower-keyed, lower-budgeted crusades led by nationals may be used very effectively to complement church planting efforts. At the time of invitation, the objective of the preacher may be to invite people to sign up for a Bible study which will start on a designated date.

◆ **The church planter should practice a reproducible style of leadership.**

From day one, even before the Bible Study begins, the leader should not do anything which cannot be reproduced by new converts soon after they are saved. (For the person who is accustomed to using direct leadership methods, this may seem far-fetched.) I would not preach a polished sermon in the midst of church planting. There will be places where direct and powerful preaching will be helpful, but not in the church planting process if we want to practice a rapid transfer of leadership.

The planter must be aware of everything he says and the way he says it because people are watching and are going to copy his words and style. What kind of prayer will be the first one heard by the members of the Bible study? If it is long, filled with pious and religious words, many new converts will not attempt to pray because they find it difficult to copy the model they have heard. The first prayer the members will hear me pray will be something like this, "Dear God, thank you for our Bible study tonight. Amen." Not even two sentences, but reproducible.

My teaching method must be reproducible. This is one of the reasons I use an indirect method of leadership wherein reliance is on the Scriptures and the Holy Spirit, not on my ability. I guide the group as they focus on the Word under the inspiration of the Holy Spirit.

Some will say any strategy or method will work; and this is true in many cases. But some strategies and methods may more likely lead to genuine faith and healthy reproducing churches. If reaching the world is important, then we must be careful to adopt strategies and methods which will allow us to be as effective as possible. Before beginning the procedure of planting churches, the planter is ahead if he knows well the strategy he will use.

Chapter 15

What Style of Leadership Will I Use?

I must ask myself what I want to see accomplished. My objectives will largely determine the kind of leadership I will use. If my objectives are to bring people to an authentic faith relationship with Christ then help them to become a church, I need to find the most effective kind of leadership which will bring about the fulfillment of these goals. There are two basic concerns which should be dealt with.

First, what is the most effective method of transmitting content so that it will be understood and personally received by the hearers?

Second, is the style of leadership easily transferable? Is it reproducible? Do I want new converts to be able to do what I have done?

For rapid and solid church growth, both of these—effectively transmitting a message and modeling a reproducible type of leadership—are of vital importance. Successful communication is more than shouting the message and hoping someone hears it. The messenger's obligation is not over until he has delivered the message in the most effective way possible.

There are two broad methods of leadership, direct and indirect.

◆ Direct Leadership

This is the most popular among preachers and teachers. This method is seen in the presentation of a sermon or lecture. It is characterized by leader-centeredness. The spotlight is on the leader. Much of the success depends on his ability to convey the message. Not just anyone can be an effective communicator of truth as the sole active participant in front of passive listeners. When practicing direct leadership, there is a need for a degree of charisma, confidence, and boldness. Special education is often needed for a person to communicate effectively by using direct leadership methods. When a person is trained to speak in college and seminary, it is sometimes difficult not to speak. This is especially true when dealing with a group of people who have no Christian background or who are nominal Christians.

Direct communication has been used very effectively through the ages to convey the Gospel message. Many churches have been planted using straightforward preaching. There are those who use a combination of both direct and indirect leadership methods. Few would use one to the exclusion of the other. Evangelistic crusades are a common example of direct leadership in church planting. One of the problems with this method is the fact that such a critical spotlight beams upon the leader. The number of people capable of this style of leadership is very limited. Many ordinary people would be disqualified to do church planting if they were expected to use this method.

◆ Indirect leadership

Indirect leadership involves guidance by the leader and participation by the group, resulting in a rapid transfer of leadership. Guidance, participation, and transfer of leadership become important concepts for the planter. In indirect leadership, the spotlight beams on the participants and the authority is the Word of God. The leader does not need to give sermonettes at every point; rather he lets the Scripture speak. The more the people are involved, the more they will learn and retain. The simple Bible study method which we will look at in detail allows the people to read, hear, think, speak, and write. The leader is very much in control, but he can be in control without speaking all the time.

With this method, the leader must trust the Word. He must be confident enough not to have to talk all the time. He must be able to joyfully and prayerfully watch people grow as the Word is brought alive by the energizing power of the Holy Spirit. Many times the Word of God is much more respected than the words of a man about the Word of God.

Through observation and experience, I have developed a special appreciation for indirect leadership in church planting. Watching my three sons study at home using correspondence courses and knowing that they were learning well told me something about indirect leadership. Our oldest son completed high school without direct leadership. Without a "teacher," he made very high marks and entered college as a sophomore. In my pastorates in the States I used direct leadership. If I dared ask the congregation the title of last week's sermon, many could not remember. To ask members to give the title and Scripture reference would have been asking a lot.

Below you will see some conclusions drawn from a study done by the United States Air Force.

How We Learn

1% through TASTE
1 1/2% through TOUCH
3 1/2% through SMELL
11% through HEARING
83% through SIGHT

METHODS OF COMMUNICATION

	Recall 3 Hours later	Recall 3 Days later
A. Telling	70%	10%
B. Showing	72%	20%
C. Telling and Showing	85%	65%

I HEAR: I FORGET   I SEE: I REMEMBER

I DO: I UNDERSTAND

In the above illustration, "telling" would correspond to a typical sermon or lecture. After three days the retention level is low; I would evaluate this as overly optimistic. If my desire is to communicate in the most effective way possible, I would want to involve the students in more than passive listening. To gain maximum communication, I will expect the students to: **hear, see, analyze,** and **do,** which may involve discussion and writing. This means that as leader I will guide the group as they participate, a participation which involves hearing, seeing, analyzing, and doing.

In church planting I have involved the Bible study members in full participation, and I am convinced there is a clear advantage in using this method.

Chapter 16

What Do You Do When There Is Little or No Response?

Not all places are equally responsive. It makes sense to primarily target responsive areas. This does not mean the Lord will not lead some to sow seeds in resistant areas. Responsiveness will often be hastened when the Gospel seed is sown. It is interesting to note that in some countries one group of missionaries will report that it is very difficult to win people to Christ and start new churches while other missionaries, maybe from another denomination, are reporting very rapid growth. It is true that in certain cultures and religious backgrounds, church growth will be slower than in others. But what am I to do if the growth is very slow? There are four areas that should be closely analyzed before concluding that an area is almost unreachable.

1. The messenger should be analyzed.

Suggesting such, especially among veteran missionaries, may be like walking through a mine field—not a friendly atmosphere. However, the Holy Spirit can prepare hearts for constructive self-analysis and this is healthy for every church planter from time to time.

♦ The **expectation level** may be the key to success or failure.

Having been in a number of missions in various countries, I have noticed some missionaries saying, "It takes ten years to get a convert here." But others in the same mission and country tell how they have won people whose lives have really been changed after a few times of sharing the Gospel Some will say it takes many years to get a church born, while others reveal how churches are born in a short period of time. There are factors in the life of the planter which will influence rapid or slow growth. One's theology as to what a church is will make a difference. A person's personality will make a difference; some are laid back and others are very aggressive. But a major factor is the expectation level. The missionary who thinks it can't be done can expect as much. The one who says it will take many years to get a church started will take many years to get a church started.

Seldom will one accomplish more that he expects. There are places where church growth has been slower than in other parts of the world. The tendency in these resistant areas is to predict the future on the basis of the past. If it has been tough for the past ten years, then it must be tough for the next ten years. This thinking requires no faith. One of the most deadly and most difficult ruts to get out of is a life-long pattern of little or no fruit. The low expectation level must be broken and new dreams dreamed.

- **Aggressiveness** makes a difference.

Sitting in an office waiting for it to happen does not get the job done. Fear of confrontation may seal the lips and stifle church growth. Sometimes this fear comes from not wanting to hurt feelings or cause loss of face, but more often it is a personal fear of losing ones own face, and a lack of a natural, spontaneous witness. If a person thinks, "It does no good, they will not respond," he will lack adequate aggression to go after the people. Boldness in sharing the Gospel characterized the lives of Peter and Paul. Paul boldly proclaimed the Gospel to the pagan Athenians, people as pagan as any culture on the face of the earth today. Can you imagine Paul hesitating to preach the Gospel because the people were hardened in a culture which knew many gods but had no place for the Lord God Jehovah? Can you imagine Paul saying, "I will preach this message, but it won't do any good." His aggressiveness opened doors which would have remained closed had he chosen to be silent and "diplomatic."

◆ Being a person of **Faith** makes a difference.

Faith to believe God to be able in all circumstances will result in much fruit. We know God will not force people to receive His Son, but He is not willing that any should perish, and woe to the church planter if the people perish due to his lack of faith. The planter must exhibit a fixed faith in the midst of fluctuating circumstances—circumstances of resistance, persecution, seed sowing, cultivating, and harvest.

2. The message must be analyzed.

The proper message spells the difference between success and failure. If the response is very slow, one should look closely at the message being communicated, if in fact it is being communicated. It made a difference in Paul's ministry. Near the end of his ministry we hear Paul saying, . . . *I only want to complete my mission and finish the work that the Lord Jesus gave me to do, which is to declare the Good News about the grace of God.* Acts 20:24 He continues in verse 27, *For I have not held back from announcing to you the whole purpose of God.* In 1 Corinthians 15:3 Paul says, *I passed on to you what I received, which is of the greatest importance: that Christ died for our sins, as written in the Scriptures; that he was buried and that he was raised to life three days later, as written in the Scriptures.* When Paul begins a letter in the New Testament he underscores his call to preach the **Good News of Jesus Christ**.

There are those who believe people to be so hard-hearted that the simple Gospel is not adequate. On the contrary, the harder the hearts and the greater the resistance, the greater the importance of proclaiming the pure, simple Gospel message. To seek other roads—social change, political change—only serves to weaken the message. Christian work ethics evolve, dignity is established, stomachs are filled, social orders are changed for the better and on a more permanent basis, only when Christ has become Lord. The Gospel message must be wrapped in love and human concern. The planter must live the message as he proclaims it if there is to be fruit.

Some say, "The simple message is not enough, it is too simple." Sin is sin in the life of the Ph.D. just as in the life of the uneducated. Romans 3:23, 26 is clear and adequate. John 3:16 has the same needed message for the senior adult as for the child. One of the clearest pictures of the full Gospel message is found in Romans 1:1-4. For the people of Thessalonica, people who were committed to idol worship, Paul knew the Gospel to be adequate. He said, *For we brought the Good News to you, not with words only, but also with power and the Holy Spirit, and with complete conviction of its truth.* I Thessalonians 1:5 In Paul's words we sense oozing confidence, the fruit of a strong conviction of the truth he proclaims.

When response is slow, the planter should carefully examine the seed being sown. Certain portions of the Scripture will be more relevant and effective in reaching the lost. The Gospel message is profound, yet simple enough for a child to understand. This is the fundamental, undiluted message essential for bringing people to faith and churches into being.

3. The methodology must be analyzed.

In a responsive area many methods will be successful in planting churches, though some will be more effective than others. The objectives should determine the methods used. There are some methods which will result in slower growth than other methods.

There is no desire to adopt a "fast" method to the detriment of healthy church planting. There are some methods which may result in very slow church planting, but the slowness of growth does not necessarily mean healthy church planting. It seems reasonable to seek methods that will result in the fastest possible multiplication of *healthy* churches.

Methods which work through social ministries or other mediating ministries may result in slower church growth than a bold head-on proclamation of the Gospel. For example, in countries where English classes form the basis for reaching people, there is likelihood that the growth will be slow. History has not generally revealed that the presence of a Christian school or hospital has greatly accelerated church growth. This is not to say these are invalid in seed sowing and cultivation. In some countries these types of doors may be the only way to get in to bear witness. However, even when the growth is slow, the missionaries should not rule out the possibility of a change of religious and political climate which will make straight-forth witnessing and preaching the best approach.

Creativity and flexibility in applying techniques and a sensitivity to the leading of the Holy Spirit are crucial.

◆ **Paul in resistant societies**

Much can be learned by a study of Paul's methods when he faced resistant and pagan societies. We see two such occasions in Acts 14 and Acts 17. A common pattern is seen on both occasions.

Lystra (Acts 14)

Polytheism abounded. The people were pagan gentiles. Paul started where the people were in their idolatry.

He used this as a basis to introduce his purpose for being there. He said, *We are here to announce the Good New.* Acts 14:15

He then introduced a living God in contrast to their lifeless idols.(v.15) Paul contextualized his message. In the midst of gods, he spoke of a powerful, yet loving God. In this agricultural area, he spoke of the ability of the true God to send needed rain and provide food.

God is introduced as: Creator (v.15); Merciful (v.17); Provider (v.17); God of history (vv.15-17).

Paul included an evangelistic appeal. In verse 15 he spoke of repentance, a turning away from the old way of life. His was a straight-forth strategy. His method met the people head on where they were in their spiritual needs, and he boldly identified the solution.

Athens (Acts 17)

These, too, were pagan gentiles. They were middle class in pursuit of intellectual heights. Note the situation and Paul's approach.

It was a polytheistic society. Paul noticed how *full of idols the city was.* v.16

Epicurean and Stoic teachers loved to debate and discuss the latest intellectual fad. (v.18)

Paul met people where they were physically and spiritually. He proclaimed this message in the synagogue and in the public square. (v. 17)

Even though it was a new teaching, a foreign religion to the hearers, Paul preached about Jesus and the resurrection. (vv.18-19) This caught their attention and opened the door for Paul to give a fuller message.

The same pattern is followed as in Lystra. The true and living God is introduced in contrast to the many lifeless gods. (v. 24)

God is pictured as: Creator (v.24); in the world yet greater than the world (v.24, 27); Lord of history (v.26, 30); a good God who sustains life (v.28); merciful (v.30); just (vv.30-31).

Paul closed with an evangelistic appeal. (vv.30-31)

Some did not believe, but some did. Paul's message did not change, even though he contextualized the message in relating it to the people. He went straight for the mind of man without apology or compromise.

Many would label these as resistant areas, and they were, but something happened when a "foolish" message was preached. Paul expected something to happen.

4. The target should be analyzed.

When growth is slow, the planter could be aiming at the wrong target. A mission may get in a rut of targeting a certain sector of society and retain that target even when there is little or no response.

If the wealthy are being targeted and there is little response, why not alter the target and concentrate on another level of society. Try the middle and lower classes. They may be responsive and we will never know unless they are intentionally a part of our target. If the white collars are not responsive, take note of massive segments of blue collars.

If a certain non-Christian religious group is very resistant, analyze other religious groups. In Bangladesh church planting flared when the target was changed from one religious group to another. In the Philippines there are resistant non-Christian groups such as the indigenous Iglesia ni Cristo and the Muslims. But others are very responsive to the Gospel.

If an old, settled, unchanging city is not responsive, what about the transient student population? What about the industrial zones ringed by semi-migrant workers?

Natural calamities and disasters, such as earthquakes, floods and drought, may make an area more targetable. When there is flux in a regional economy or political unrest, this may signify a greater openness to the Gospel.

Proper targeting may spell the difference between slow growth and rapid growth. The church planter must be able to adjust targets. Aiming at targets which can be hit makes for better planting.

It is not for any of us to judge those who are working among a resistant people. It is a blessing to see such workers always trying to do a more effective job of church planting. It is important that these do not resign themselves to the expectation that, because of little response in years past, there will be little response today and tomorrow. A thorough examination of the **Messenger,** the **Message,** the **Methods,** and the **Masses** must be done before anyone can authoritatively say, "The response is so slow and so little."

Little response does not necessarily mean failure on the part of the messenger or the message. There are some people who will never believe. Some turned away in unbelief in the presence of God's own Son.

Chapter 17

Clearance From Community Officials to Have a Bible Study

In some parts of the world this is not applicable, but in some nations these are cultural considerations which must be dealt with. In the Philippines one must decide what to do concerning the barrio captain, for the captain is the head political official in the barrio. He is chosen by the people of the barrio and has a great deal of respect. In many ways he is in charge of the barrio. (A barrio may be a very small village or it may include a large population.) In the rural areas the captain may be more visible and more powerful.

The church planter has three options; go straight to the captain and seek clearance for a Bible study, ignore him, or simply announce the time of the meeting and invite him to attend. We must remember the purpose of the Bible study is not political or to raise money. If it were either of these, it would be very proper to seek the permission of the captain and perhaps other officials. Using a barrio owned building would necessitate getting special permission. The Bible study is a community meeting, but it is being sponsored by one or more families in the community.

Consider the options:

◆ **Going to the officials to get permission.**

If the captain or officials are not sympathetic, they may say no and that would be the end of it. The door would be closed and it would be very difficult to proceed with a Bible study. Usually the community leaders will not understand the nature or purpose of the Bible study, especially if they are of a religion that may be hostile toward other religions. One of the ways a barrio captain would react in the Philippines if he does not want the Bible study is to say, "Let me take this up with my councilmen, and I will let you know." This is an Asian way of saying no. If you go back and ask him the results of the meeting with the councilmen he may say, "They think it is good, but we should wait until another time because the people are so busy." This often means a closed door and it would be foolish to ignore the community leaders and try to continue with the Bible study.

◆ **Not asking permission from the barrio captain or community officials.**

This option may violate cultural norms enough to create unnecessary opposition from the beginning. On the other hand, in some large barrios, especially in urban areas, a community Bible study held at a person's house may not suffer at all if the officials are not contacted or even invited.

◆ **Notifying the barrio captain of the beginning date and place and inviting him to attend.**

This would be my position most of the time. The date is set, the place is determined, invitations are given out. I would then go with some of the sponsors of the Bible study to meet the community leaders to let them know what we are doing and give them a special invitation to attend. In this way culture is not violated. The officials are given proper respect, yet are not allowed to get in a position to stop the Bible study before it ever begins.

High-rise apartments, condominiums, mobile home parks often require getting permission from management unless you already have tenants to host a Bible study.

Chapter 18

Promotion and Invitations

I prefer to get the people involved, as much as possible, in every aspect of the church planting process. Often there are one or more families who are willing to sponsor or host the Bible study. In getting people to attend the initial Bible Study, I depend heavily on the ones sponsoring or hosting it. Since it is to be a community Bible study, it is imperative that the community be invited. This is done by personal invitations, friends to friends. Written invitations and notices are used. I will get with the hosts and work with them in making small signs to be placed in strategic areas. (Heavy art paper works well and is usually available.) Also, we will fill out hundreds of small leaflets. I have these made up in large quantities, thus keeping the price in a reproducible range. The leaflet may look like this:

A SPECIAL HOUR JUST FOR YOU
(For adults and teens)

BIBLE STUDY   **MUSIC**

WHEN?_____

WHERE?_____

HOUR?_____

Led by:_____(Bible Teacher)

EVERY ONE WELCOME

Normally, this is the extent of the promotion I use in getting a group for the initial Bible Study. The leaflets are given out a day or two before the first meeting. Those hosting the Bible study often are the key in getting others to attend.

SECTION III

THE CHURCH PLANTING PROCESS

Chapter 19

The Pre-Salvation Stage

Churches may be born by gathering scattered believers. This is legitimate church planting. In some places there is an influx of people for various reasons. In nations where there are many believers, this influx will include some believers who need a new church home.

Churches may be born when a small nucleus of believers consciously band together for the express purpose of enlarging the group through community or home Bible studies. (Some call these cell groups.) This also is a very legitimate way to plant churches.

Churches may be born when a group or person with abundant financial resources, comes into a place and rents a large theater or auditorium as a meeting place. The ingredients for this kind of church planting, if it is to be successful, include not only a special kind of building which is very comfortable, but a professional, charismatic preacher/leader. There should be accomplished musicians with a band or orchestra. A very good public address system is required. There will be overhead projectors for use in congregational singing. The question is how this proposed mega church will quickly fill up such a large and expensive place. This method of church planting is not nearly as successful where there are few or no believers. It is not necessary to have a place to seat 1000 if you do not have believers to start with. Solid growth does not normally come this quickly, so something else must be done. It often happens like this: The place is a city where there is a large number of small community churches of various faiths. These small churches are pastored by local men, some good preachers, some not so good. Many of them are bivocational. The small churches may have 20 to 200 in Sunday attendance. Some are struggling. All have fringe, disgruntled members and some members who would be tempted by a more comfortable setting and professional performance. By this time you can guess how this mega church blossoms overnight. Proselyting is the name of the game in many cases.

As a few of these large entertaining churches come into being, church hopping becomes a favorite past time for many people. Everything from good preaching to rock-style music with a disco atmosphere draws the people.

The result looks good and some of it is, but what of the lesser lights, the community pastors whose struggles have intensified because of membership drainage? (There is nothing wrong in churches becoming big; we need them. The question is how they become big. Some do it with solid spiritual births and some through proselyting.) There is almost no such thing as an instant mega church that comes through legitimate growth.

A variation of the last example is the planting of a church by church splits. This is one of the few ways of "instant church" with a large group to begin with. Either the pastor or someone else takes a sizable percentage of the membership of the "mother" church and uses these people to form a nucleus for starting another church. There is no problem with a nucleus of members going out from a church to begin a new work if it is done with the blessing of the church.

Some of the above ways of starting churches are acceptable, notably the first two. There is a third way which I have experienced exclusively through the years. One of my favorite church planting verses is found in Romans 15:20 and sheds light on my personal philosophy of church planting. Paul said, *My ambition has always been to proclaim the Good News in places where*

Christ has not been heard of, so as not to build on a foundation laid by someone else.

The greatest need today is for the birth of churches through bringing people to Christ and then guiding them into church consciousness. When the objective is a fully indigenous church, I have found it best not to begin with transferees or half committed believers. I prefer to begin with new converts who are free of tradition, especially if that tradition is contrary to New Testament and indigenous principles. The best way to hinder the birth and development of an indigenous church is to have a few members who have been spoiled by outside help to the point that the recipients have been rendered helpless dependents.

Chapter 20

Salvation: The First Objective

Only as salvation is taken very seriously can one expect to be successful in planting churches. It is at this point where many fail. Therefore we will look at the Biblical concept of salvation for a moment. It is amazing how routine and watered down the concept of salvation has become, not only in theory, but even more in practical application. Well-intentioned, highly-educated missionaries often have been lulled to sleep and treat salvation too lightly.

There is a great deal of discussion about the back door problem of our churches. So many come in only to go out the back door almost unnoticed. I am convinced it is not a back door problem as much as it is a front door problem. Some will say we just need better follow up, and there is no doubt about that. But if strong and healthy churches are to be planted, a proper understanding of salvation must be held by the church planter. Great care should be taken to choose a strategy or method of communication of the Gospel which assures the reaching of this objective as much as possible. Most any method will work part of the time to some degree, but when the final product hangs in the balance, it is imperative that the planter examine and choose the method which most effectively communicates the Gospel that leads to new life.

There are areas of the world where the people are very open and quickly make decisions. In many developing nations an American preaching a strong message will find it easy to get scores of decisions; yet if one knows the culture and religious background, he will know that many will make decisions for reasons other than the salvation the foreigner is talking about. Quite often it is a joke when presumptuous foreigners come in and quickly win so many to Christ. It is amazing how well a foreigner can fully "understand" the culture in one week while many missionaries still try to figure it out after many years of living in the land. One crusade leader complained that the missionaries must not be doing anything since he could win more to Christ in a week than they win in a year. At a victory banquet following a week-long crusade in Manila, one fellow gave this testimony. "I went house to house and met the families. I would tell them, 'What I have to share is too important to share with just a few. Go invite neighbors in and I will tell you the good news.' In no time, there would be twenty people in the house and in fifteen minutes all of them were saved and I just kept doing this all day long." A person who has lived in Manila and knows the culture and religion will know this was Asian hospitality. But it goes on and on with the blessing of sending agencies and is endured by local missionaries who know that often it is a game, a fatal one. Cheap grace has become such a common feature of the American religious scene that imported preachers often transfer what they know and have practiced at home. This is not enough in a pagan culture that often strives to please the guest at any cost.

How do many preachers approach getting people saved? For a moment let us go to a typical evangelistic meeting. The preacher preaches a good sermon. He gives an invitation for people to make a decision. Assume the crowd is made up of nominal Christians who know little about the Bible, even though they may have great respect for it. They may even know about Christ and have a great deal of respect for Him. They may also believe that one has to do good works and go through many religious rituals in order to be put right with God. They may believe Mary to be the mother of God and co-redemptress. The preacher asks everyone who wants to go to heaven to raise their hands. Most hands go up since everyone wants to go to heaven someday. Then with the people trapped, the preacher asks for all those who raised their hands to come to the front. The people do not know what is going to happen at the front when they go forward. Some may think there will be a free sack of rice. Others may go just to please the guest speaker. Some may go so they can create a position wherein the speaker becomes indebted to them for doing his bidding. It is a simple game of social security that works like this. Every time a person can please or do something for someone else, it is like putting something in the bank. In the evangelistic service the speaker becomes indebted to the one who did something for him, which was going forward.

Those who respond to the invitation are greeted by the preacher, pastor, or some counselor. The preacher may say something like this: "Welcome, we are glad you came tonight. Do you want to receive Christ as your Savior?" "Yes," the person says. "Do you believe that you are a sinner?" Again, the answer is yes. "Do you want to go to heaven when you die?" Again, it is yes. "Do you believe that Jesus died on the cross for you and that He was raised from the grave?" Yes, is the answer. "Will you pray this prayer after me?" Yes, again. The preacher does not ask the seeker to pray since it might be too difficult and may embarrass him. So the preacher prays and asks the person to repeat what he says. After the prayer the preacher gives a hearty handshake and joyfully announces that the seeker now is a child of God and on his way to heaven. He may ask the seeker, "Do you feel better?" and quickly states to those observing, "I know he does; look at that smile on his face." Can you imagine Jesus using this approach? This is easy believism and cheap grace.

There is no doubt that some really are saved in such situations, but in church planting you do not want a group where one or two out of twenty are really saved. This is the back door problem some talk about. We "get them in" and wonder why they don't stay.

Go back to the counseling session for a moment. What if the preacher asks questions like this: Are you a sinner? Do you believe that Christ is the Savior of the world? Do you believe that Mary is co-redemptress and Mother of God? In Mexico City or Manila the answer will be yes to all of the above questions. This raises the question of whether a person can be saved when having more than one object of saving faith. Acts 4:12 says no; it must be Christ alone.

When my family went to the Philippines, we had a young woman working for us in our home. She came from a religious background which allowed her to know in general about God, Jesus, Mary, etc. But she had no concept of what it meant to be saved. She thought she was a Christian because of her infant baptism and the accumulation of good works. Our prayer was that through exposure to the Bible she would come to know Christ in a real and personal way. She proved to be stubborn. No doubt she had received warnings from home about this new religion of her employers. After many months she began attending an evangelical church with her friends. Week after week I would ask her if anything had happened during the worship service. One day she said, "Yes, something happened today." I quickly asked what it was and she replied, "After the preacher preached, an invitation was given for those who wanted to accept Christ to come forward. I felt as if a hand was pushing me to go to the front, so I did." "Then what happened," I asked? She said, "They gave me a card, and asked me to sit down and fill it out." "Then what?" "We all stood at the front and the preacher took the cards and gave our names and then people came by and shook hands with us." "Then what?" I asked. "That was all," she said. Cheap grace?

By the time this conversation took place her guard was firmly up again and we never found another time when it could be penetrated. The young woman later married and moved away.

One day my wife and I went to visit her and see her new baby. As she left the baby in the room she was careful to pin a cross on the gown so the baby would be protected. She was so close, but never again to be open to the Gospel in the same way as she was on that potentially eventful Sunday morning. The preacher was sincere, highly educated, but perhaps in the higher levels where education had taken him, he could not deal with the subject of salvation in a real, serious way. Cheap grace abounds from fear of hurting feelings and from a desire to be successful.

From this true story we are reminded that searching, hoping, is not the same as finding. Inquiring is not the same as acquiring. The rich young ruler ran to Jesus with the right questions, with sincerity, searching, but he went away lost. A person putting up a hand indicating that he wants to follow Jesus is not necessarily the same as following Jesus. People may come forward to find out, to inquire, but they often need help in knowing what they are to do and how to do it. The man who asks, "What must I do to be saved?" is not saved until he repents of his sin and trusts Jesus Christ as his Savior.

How does all this relate to indigenous church planting? It relates to the very core of it, for if we slip up at this point, there is nothing more to do in church planting.

Salvation is of greatest importance if the church planter sees people as lost when they do not know Christ as personal Savior. The planter must know that people are eternally lost without Christ. When conducting church planting seminars in one country, I found that the normal number of new churches planted by that group in an entire year is four to six. As I visited with missionaries and tried to understand why the growth was so slow, I found several contributing factors. The materialistic and religious climate was no small factor, but the problem may have been more in the theology of some of those who should have been planting churches. It was in the area of salvation. A missionary who had spent a lifetime in the country said the biggest problem was universalism, a doctrine that saturates pastors and higher institutions of learning. To the universalist, sin is not serious, therefore the cross fades into insignificance. It was no surprise to learn that those pastors don't give an invitation. If people are not lost, why give an invitation?

If missionaries and pastors do not see people as lost eternally unless they receive Christ and Him alone, there is no hope for rapid church planting or growth. As I was lecturing in a missions class in a major seminary in the United States, a young man stood up and scolded me because I seemed to be saying that a person devoted in his religion may be lost if he has not been born again. He said, "Don't you know that we are in the ecumenical era and that those people are our brothers?" (With this kind of theological climate, it was not a surprise when in another class another young man stood up and told me that what I was saying was offensive. He said, "You seem to be saying that one must believe in the virgin birth to be a Christian.")

If a person is going to heaven anyway, with or without faith in Christ, there is no urgency, not even a need to proclaim the Gospel and plant churches. Theology does make a difference in church planting.

The church planter must help the unsaved to understand they are lost. Until a person is lost, he cannot be found. Only when one knows he is guilty of the sin of rejecting God's only Son, can he repent of that sin, the sin that condemns him. The Good News can be Good News only when a person understands and feels responsible for his sinful position. It is not enough to tell a person that God loves him. It is not enough only to tell a person to believe. Unless the carrier of the Good News points out the sin problem, it is not likely a person will ever understand it and feel guilty. A theological concept of salvation that takes lightly sin and repentance may produce a religious group but not a true church.

In Asia, loss of face is something to be avoided, even at great cost. People kill simply over loss of face. But unless a person comes to a total loss of face, he can never go to heaven. Repentance is an absolute necessity before a person can know Christ. Repentance means admitting that, up to this point, I have been wrong in my attitudes and actions toward God. It involves a deep sorrow and turning away from one kind of life to embrace another. It's the end of passing the buck. The old personal self must die. This is painful, but without it, there is no healing.

The tendency is to try to make people feel good, even if it means ignoring sin and its consequences. Some will try to excuse themselves by blaming culture and allowing culture to supersede the Bible in standard setting.

Many evangelicals confront people with a partial Gospel, the believe and receive part, and ignore the lordship part. When witnessing or counseling with someone, we use such verses as Romans 3:23; Romans 10:9-10; John 1:12; 3:15-18,36; Ephesians 2:8-9; John 5:24; and a few others. These are great verses to use in leading a person to saving faith in Christ, but there is more.

How did Jesus approach the subject of salvation?

We see His approach in John 3 when he tells a religious leader that his physical birth into a Jewish religion was not enough and if he expected to ever see heaven, he would have to have a radical change that could come only from above. He said it would be so revolutionary it would be like having a complete new start, a new birth. It was a tough approach, calling for a total change in lifestyle.

Again, we see His approach in Mark 10:17-22. To the rich young ruler He said that if the young man wanted to be His disciple, he must demonstrate that Christ was number one in all of his living. Jesus challenged him to demonstrate his love and commitment by selling all he had and giving it to the poor. Jesus was saying it was all or nothing. The young man went away lost, because he failed the test.

When addressing a crowd as recorded in Luke 14:25-33, Jesus told of the necessity of counting the cost **before** following Him. He was talking to people who were interested but had not made a firm decision. Jesus gives illustrations of the instances in life when it is only reasonable for a person to look closely at what he is getting into before beginning. He concludes in verse 33: *"In the same way," concluded Jesus, "None of you can be my disciple unless he gives up everything he has."*

Jesus talked about Lordship when He confronted people with the Gospel. A man once said to me, "Won't you run people off if you talk to them about Lordship before they are saved?" Of course, some will turn back, just as happened in the experiences of Jesus. But to get genuine converts in less number is so much better than getting a few converts mixed in with a lot of false converts.

The full Gospel will include a message about sin and the love of God as manifested in Christ's death and resurrection. It must include man's necessary response to God's invitation. It is a response of faith in the finished Work of Christ. It is a surrender of all a person knows about himself to all of Christ that he knows. It is a surrender that requires repentance of the sin of unbelief. It is a surrender that involves the will, emotions, and body.

The church planter must come to the conclusion that salvation is the beginning point of church planting and without it, or to minimize it, leaves no place to go. The planter must decide not only the method of communication, but also the particular portion of Scripture that best brings a group of people to genuine saving faith.

In my experience, which is shared by countless others in many nations, I have found **prolonged exposure to the Word** is the best way to assure that people make genuine decisions. The Gospel of John has been my choice of Scripture to use in bringing the salvation message to the lost.

At this time we will examine closely a technique of Bible study using *Good News For You* based on the Gospel of John. This method of Bible study will allow a prolonged exposure to the Word of God, bringing people to a saving faith in Christ.

Chapter 21

One Technique Illustrated

We will now look closely at a simple technique which I have found to be effective in rural areas, and even more effective in urban settings. Let me emphasize that, while this is one method that works, it is not the only one. This is not the only method I have used. It is not **the** way, it is **a** way. It is a basic tool which can be altered as the Holy Spirit leads in differing circumtances. It is important that a church planter know and feel comfortable with one simple and reproducible technique, then flexibility and experimentation can follow. There are some who spend much time in study and theorizing and never prove any method to be effective.

We must embrace some basic principles and at least one method. **The prolonged exposure of the receptive heart to the Word of God is a fundamental which cannot be by-passed if we hope to have healthy, New Testament churches.** This is the fundamental that we will now examine closely.

The time frame will vary from country to country and from one religious group to another. Some will say a seven week span is a long time to deal with the topic of salvation. Others will say this is a very short time. A number of factors influence the time frame, the most important being religious background and respect for the Bible.

Introduction Night

We are assuming the church planting is being done in an area where there is a degree of openness and interest. This means it is possible to get a group of ten or more together for the Bible study. (The approach and technique will work as well with the cluster approach where there are several groups which are much smaller.) It is important to remember we are to allow the Holy Spirit to lead us to responsive and prepared people. To get a group of curious people together using entertainment come-ons is not what I am talking about. To follow that idea will result in a rapid dropout rate simply because the people were not deeply interested and thirsty. **Rapid church growth will depend on finding the Holy Spirit-prepared soil.**

Preliminaries completed

All of the "home work" has been done. Much prayer and preparation have preceded this point. The place, day, and time have been set. The Bible study has been publicized. The church planter needs to take the following with him on introduction night:

One copy each of *Good News For You*, **Gospel of John, Song booklet, Bible, sign up sheet, and some tracts.**

Remember, it is introduction night. This is a crucial night; it can make or break the Bible study. This is a time when the people meet the Bible teacher and learn more about his purpose, but also they learn about the purpose and nature of the study. It is a night when the people will be disarmed, their suspicions and fears allayed. When this is done, they will feel free to invite more people to attend the opening lesson.

When it appears most of the people have arrived, I will get a signal from the host that it is time to begin. Without introduction, I will begin singing a song in the language of the people. This gets the attention of the people and centers the focus on the leader. (If you cannot sing, you may want to take a small cassette player and play the opening song. If you are working in a team, perhaps one of the other members will open with a song.) Since it is introduction night, I choose not to teach songs to the group.

The leader should know exactly what he is going to do and why he is going to do it. If you are among a large group of strangers, it is no time to be unsure of yourself. In the Philippines it is not unusual to have someone present who comes with the purpose of causing division and confusion. The larger the group, the more likely this is to happen. Trouble makers usually come from two religious groups which are cultic in nature. If one stands and asks the name of my religion, I can be fairly sure it is someone from "Iglesia ni Cristo," an indigenous cult of the Philippines. If someone stands and asks the name of God, it is probably someone from the Jehovah's Witnesses. Disturbance seems to be more likely in the province when you have larger groups meeting in public places. This does not happen often, so the Bible study leader need not go in fear, but must be prepared and alert. The introduction should be smooth flowing without unnecessary pauses or interruptions.

The following outline is suggested:

1. Open with a song if desirable

2. Bible study leader introduces self

I will say something like this, "I am Charles Brock, a Bible teacher from San Fernando. I have lived there for the past twelve years. I have a wife and three sons. We came to the Philippines in 1971. My work is to teach the Bible to whoever wants to learn more about it."

3. Leader introduces his purpose

Negative
"I am not here to debate or philosophize, and we will not do it. If your purpose in being here is to debate with me, please meet me immediately after the close of the meeting. We will set a time for you to come to my house tomorrow where we will talk as long as you want, all day if you like."

If there are such people present, it is important to close the door firmly at the very beginning. So as not to cause loss of face, I will gently open the door, but the time and venue is another. Usually people who want to spend time debating or philosophizing are not in pursuit of truth, rather they want to expose their intelligence or cause confusion. If they debate, they want an audience.

Positive
"My purpose is to share the Good News about Jesus Christ as found in the Bible, the Word of God."

4. Illustration of a person who was searching for Good News

"There is a story in the Bible about a man who was like you; he was seeking the truth about life. We read this story in John's Gospel, chapter three, verses one through twenty-one." At this time I will read the entire story in the language of the hearers.

Then I will say, "Maybe you are like Nicodemus. Would you like to learn more of what the Bible says about the good life that leads to heaven? How many want to continue this study?" At this point, hands go up indicating a desire to continue. I will make a few comments about Nicodemus, but feel no need to "preach."

5. Introduction of subject matter

I will introduce the group to the Gospel of John and explain that it is a part of the Bible. The seven lesson booklet *Good News For You* is introduced. From this booklet I will read a question, such as the second question in lesson one, *Jesus called Himself the_____ of the World.* John 8:12 I will then read John 8:12 and usually the people are able to fill in the blank when I repeat the question. The people are assured that this is the nature of the entire study. They are told that the lessons are neither Roman Catholic, Jewish, nor Protestant, but are simply questions and all the answers must come directly from the Bible. I make a commitment that I will not philosophize or impose my personal doctrines on them if they will make the same commitment.

There is a commitment that the lessons are for seven weeks only and will last for only one hour once a week.

These commitments are important since the people are busy and may be only slightly sympathetic at this point.

6. Commitment to continue made by the people

I ask for a show of hands for those who want to continue the next week. After they indicate a desire to continue, I ask all of them age thirteen and older to enroll. I ask that each enrollee write his name and age on a piece of paper I brought for that purpose.

My target is adults and teens, therefore I will strongly emphasize that those who are teenagers and older may enroll. Care is taken to explain the reason for this limitation. It is explained that the material is designed for the adult mind, but later on there may be classes for the children.

The reasons for enrollment are stated.

• So I can know how many of the **Gospels of John** and *Good News For You* to bring next week.

• So I can learn your name and get to know you personally.

• To indicate your desire to share in this study. You are not joining a new religion.

It is very important to be fully above board and transparent. The confidence of the people has not been gained and suspicion and questions are still present.

7. Enrollment

If the group is large, it is good to have several sheets of paper for enrolling. If you have only one, it will take too long for everyone to sign his name and give his age.

It is good to involve group members every time possible. You may ask for someone to assist in getting the names. Usually someone will volunteer to assist.

8. When the enrollment is finished, singing is introduced

I will ask, "Do you like to sing?" The response is always positive. I show the song booklet and tell them next week we will learn some songs.

9. Good night until next week

I do not say, "Do you have any questions?" I do not want questions at this point. The right questions are going to be asked and answered beginning next week and all the answers will come from the Scripture.

I bid them good night and say, "Come back next week and invite someone to come with you. Be sure to bring a pen or pencil. As you leave, please take this tract with you."

The above outline for introduction night will take about 35 minutes. It is only an icebreaker and introduction.

I will take care that everything I do on this night and the succeeding nights can be reproduced easily and immediately by those who come to know Christ as Savior and Lord.

What ifs....

◆ **What if** only children come for the meeting.

Always remember the objectives. It is difficult and slow to plant churches using children. Since I want as broad a base as possible to begin with, it is important that a good number of adults are in attendance. If there are three adults and ten children, I will remind them that the content of the material is for adults and we will begin next week if they can get X number of adults to come. I may say twelve or twenty. There is no magical number, but I know three is not an adequate number if there is to be rapid and strong church growth. (There are cultures where three or four may be all you can get to come. If this is so, then go with it.)

◆ **What if** the same thing happens the next week?

I will postpone starting for another week. After about three times I will talk with them about trying it again at a later time when more are interested. I will leave tracts and reading material with the three and go to another area where there is better potential for planting a church. This is not to say a few are not important to the Kingdom of God. It is saying that our goal goes beyond salvation, it reaches to the birth of a new family, a church.

◆ **What if** someone wants to debate or philosophize?

First, be sure that you have stated publicly the ground rules for the Bible study. In the introduction you have said the purpose is not to debate or philosophize. If a person asks a question that is irrelevant—it may or may not be controversial—you may commend him for the question by saying, "That is a good question, but if you don't mind, we will wait to discuss it since it is going to be a part of our study in a later lesson." Usually, if the person is sincere, he will be satisfied with this. No matter who wins a debate, you lose; so don't debate.

I remember a time when members of a Bible study group warned me that some Jehovah's Witnesses were coming for the purpose of causing a disturbance. This was back in the mountains where anyone walking would be carrying lanterns or oil lights. We would be able to see their lights as they came down the trail. We made preparation for their coming. One of the Bible study members was a government agricultural worker. He was well educated and had the gift of gab. I told the group we would watch for the coming of the intruders and when they neared the opposite side of the house, we would stand and sing the Philippine national anthem. I asked the government worker to then stand and speak on the topic of loyalty to the nation. We waited and they came down the side of the mountain. When they got within hearing distance we stood and as loudly as possible sang the national anthem. They never came around the side of the house. I don't know where they went, but they must have felt they were going to the wrong meeting.

Be prepared; be alert; but don't live in fear of such happenings. I have had one or two groups closed down because of such disturbances. But usually the interference is not as severe as the above illustration and can be dealt with in such a way that no one loses much face.

◆ **What if** the host has a change of mind and does not really want the Bible study?

Strong pressures from family, peers, and religious leaders can cause a person to back out of hosting the Bible study. Also, the person may not have understood fully the nature and purpose of the Bible study and, after some thought, realize he has gotten into something he didn't want to get into.

For example, I talk with a fellow and he is very open and appears to be ready to host a Bible study. He has a perfect place, a large covered area at the side of his house. It is public yet semi-private. The normal invitations are given out. I go there early and wait. But the host does not come out of his house to meet me. I know he is inside watching television. I wait and no one comes. From this I have learned that no one is coming because the host has not encouraged anyone to come and may have even discouraged them from coming. He has had a change of mind and it's over.

THE FIVE ITEMS NEEDED FOR THE BIBLE STUDY

1. The Bible
Let the people examine the Bible as much as they want so they can see that it is not cultic literature.

2. Gospel of John or New Testament
You will want to explain that this is exactly the same as the Gospel of John found in the Bible.

The Gospel of John is sort of an "appetizer," a glimpse into the Bible. After the people begin to see God's truths in it, their appetites will be whetted to the extent that they will be willing to buy their own Bibles. (If anyone owns a Bible it is all right for them to bring it to the study.)

3. *Good News For You*
The purpose of these seven lessons based on the Gospel of John is to bring people to authentic salvation. Each lesson will take an hour or less to complete. Each participant needs a Gospel of John and a copy of this booklet. After a church is born, the members, having been brought to salvation through this study, can then use it as a tool for evangelism. Every believer can easily use it to bring others to salvation.

Contents of *Good News For You*:
- Lesson 1 - Man's Problem
- Lesson 2 - God's Solution For Man's Problem
- Lesson 3 - Man's Response
- Lesson 4 - A Man Who Wanted New Life
- Lesson 5 - The Only Way to Heaven
- Lesson 6 - The Bridge of Life
- Lesson 7 - The Road to Life

When using *Good News For You* by indirect methods, there are some things worth noting:

♦ The planter must know that the Word of God has power to bring conversion.

♦ This method is reproducible by new converts.

♦ The principle that everybody is somebody is learned early, thus preparing for a new church composed of priests.

- People learn self-feeding from the Scriptures.

- People learn to analyze the Scriptures for themselves.

- More is learned from:
  - Asking a relevant question;
  - Finding the answer in the Bible;
  - Reading the verses;
  - Writing the answer.

- Each lesson is designed to accomplish a specific objective.

- The lessons are progressive in:
  - Length of time necessary to complete;
  - Depth of understanding;
  - Arriving at a decision.

- It is important to understand that seed must be allowed necessary time to germinate, thus one lesson each week.

- The unbeliever should not be over-fed. Digestion of intake is important, so don't try to feed steak (lessons 4-7) until the unbeliever has had time to digest milk (lessons 1-3).

- Side issues and philosophical questions should not be allowed to cut the sequential thoughts of a lesson. (These questions can be dealt with on a personal basis or at a later time.)

- The leader of the Bible study does not preach or lecture, but guides the group in their participation.

4. Song book or song sheets

Gospel songs play a significant part in conveying the salvation message. Care should be taken to teach songs that have a relevant message concerning salvation. Light-hearted praise songs may not be so relevant if the group does not know Christ as Savior. Songs of substance should be primary. I have given serious attention to putting together small song booklets with a balanced theology that meets the people where they are. These song booklets contain up to forty songs. I suggest the booklet because large song books are too expensive to be used at this stage of the church planting process. We also prepared a cassette to be used in teaching the songs. It was left with the people during the week so they could learn and practice the new songs. I do not suggest overhead projectors in areas where it is cost prohibitive. After a church is born the group can purchase this item if they want it and can afford it. Song sheets are another option, being inexpensive and reproducible.

5. Tracts

Tracts are given out on introduction night and every night throughout the seven weeks. Tracts should be heavily Scripture oriented. A name of a religion or denomination should not be on the tracts. In many areas of church planting, the presence of such a name renders the tracts almost useless. People do not want or need denominationalism as much as they need the Word. The tracts are given out following the study of each lesson.

LESSON ONE - second week

You should anticipate the attendance to be greater than on introduction night, so take extra materials. Assuming 15 people enrolled, be sure you have:

1. **A Bible** (If working with Roman Catholics and Protestants, take both Catholic and Protestant Bibles.)

2. Twenty or more copies of the **Gospel of John**

3. Twenty copies of *Good News For You*

4. Twenty copies of a small **song booklet** or **song sheet**

5. Enough **tracts** to allow every person in attendance to have one.

Begin with music

It depends on the group's aptitude for singing, but I usually teach three or four songs on the first night. This means repeating some of them more than once. If the leader cannot sing, he may have a cassette made for use throughout the church planting process. It is good to depend on the hosts for the provision of the cassette player. Even in remote and undeveloped areas, someone in the group will probably have one. The more you let the people provide those things, the easier it will be for them to continue meeting needs, even after a church is born. I would suggest not taking a cassette player or any other musical instrument. If the people want to provide such, let it be. The new church will tend to become overly dependent on such equipment all too soon. After the singing, take up the song booklets and give them to the one chosen by the group to be responsible for them.

Beginning lesson one

Even though you have introduced the materials and the nature of the study on introduction night, it will be necessary to do it again. It is very likely you will have several new people who were not present on introduction night. You will need to explain clearly how the study will be conducted.

You may want to read the instructions on the inside cover of *Good News For You.* This will help the people to see that all who desire may participate in the reading of the questions and the Scripture verses. Everyone is encouraged to participate.

It is important to state clearly that anyone who does not want to read is under no pressure to do so. In some groups there will be those who cannot read or cannot see well enough to read. The leader must be sensitive to these and make them feel a part of the group even though they do not read.

The very important theme of **"everybody is somebody"** is practiced here. The church planter knows that in the future this concept is going to be of utmost importance in the development of a church where every member is expected to be an active, full-time minister.

Two possible approaches:

1. It depends on the size of the group, but the leader may ask for **volunteer**s to read. This is okay as long as one or two do not dominate. In a large group I do not know, I will usually use this method.

2. **Row by row,** people take turns reading. This is the best way to assure full participation. The leader clearly states that it is okay if anyone doesn't want to read. This method is very easy to use when the leader knows the participants and knows that there is no one who will be embarrassed by not being able to read.

Depending on the nature and size of the group, the leader may want to remain standing all the way through the lesson. Until the leader gets to know the people, it is better to maintain a tighter control of the situation. There is something about his standing that symbolizes authority and control. (Later when he knows the group and is not concerned that some will try to take control or disrupt, he can sit and relax as he guides the group in the study.)

The leader will ask someone to read the first question. It is important that everyone hear the question. If the reader doesn't speak loudly enough, don't hesitate to ask him to repeat it more loudly. The people then find the chapter and verse in the Gospel of John. From this verse they will find the answer. The leader makes sure that everyone finds the verse before anyone is allowed to read. After all have found the verse, the leader asks someone to read it aloud. After the verse has been read, the leader asks for the answer. The leader does not give the answer; he will wait as long as it takes for the people to find it. If the people have trouble finding the answer, the leader may repeat the question and ask someone to read the verse again.

If the members are unfamiliar with the Bible, the first lesson will require more time to complete and more patience on the part of the leader. The education level will make a difference in the ability of the people to become acquainted with the use of the Bible. (Don't be discouraged if the first lesson seems chaotic as the people learn to find the Scripture references. This will usually be mastered during the first lesson, then the following lessons will go more smoothly.)

The leader guides the members as they participate in the Bible study. Since the material is programmed to move the mind in a predetermined path, it is not necessary for the leader to sermonize at any point. This will be his greatest temptation, but he must believe that two great, capable forces are at work, the Word of God and the Holy Spirit.

At the end of the lesson the leader may ask, "Do you have any questions about our lesson tonight?" In most groups it is very important to ask the question in this way. You do not want just any question. Remember that the lessons are progressive, dealing with the topics that need to be dealt with in proper order. (An unsaved person does not know the questions that need to be answered as much as the planter does.) If you entertain questions which are not relevant to the lesson, you will do several things. First, you have diverted the attention of the people from the main lesson you wanted them to learn that first night. If you spend forty-five minutes dealing with the topic of sin and its consequences and then spend the next thirty minutes on another topic, what will the people carry home with them? You have allowed a good question to break the sequential thought patterns you had hoped to develop. Second, if you answer irrelevant questions honestly you may erect barriers in the minds of the members much too early and unnecessarily. Third, in one sitting you may not be able to satisfactorily answer the question in such a way as to give the people a clear understanding. Fourth, you will take much more than the one hour that you have agreed upon. I usually will not ask for any questions after the first lesson. If I do, the parameters of the questions will be set by me.

An invitation will not be given after lesson one. In this lesson we have dealt only with sin. There is much the unbeliever must understand before he is ready to make a responsible decision. I can patiently wait for the eyes of his understanding to be opened by the Holy Spirit under prolonged exposure to the Gospel.

The memory verse is introduced.

At the end of each lesson there is a verse of Scripture which is a theme verse for the lesson. All the members are challenged to memorize the verse before the next meeting.

I will bid the people good night and encourage them to bring a friend next week. Each person will be given a relevant tract.

What ifs...

◆ **What if** the people forget their pens or pencils?

If it is a community Bible study within walking distance of their homes, permit them to return home to get a pen. Otherwise, encourage people to share. You may have two or three pencils they can borrow for the evening, but don't provide them with pencils each time. This may seem like a very small what if, but it does happen. Letting the people provide their own pens or pencils is a tiny first step in self-support.

◆ **What if** one person wants to read all the questions and Scripture verses or wants to give all the answers?

A simple reminder that we want everyone to take turns may be enough. If a person persists, there are two things you can do. When facing the group, you, as leader, turn away from the one dominating and ask someone from another area to read the next question. The leader can eventually turn back to face the area where this person is located. Another way to deal with the problem is to move down the row letting the people take turns one after the other. Both of these ways will allow the person who wants to dominate to participate as one of the group. Care must be taken not to hurt feelings, but it is necessary to allow everybody to be somebody. Often, this problem comes from someone who has more Biblical training or exposure than the other members. Sometimes such a person just wants to reveal his "intelligence." Sometimes it is out of a sincere desire to help the others who are not as fortunate as he. Whether it is in this stage or later in the birth of the church, the most dangerous person may be the one who has to talk all the time.

◆ **What if** a person asks a question that is irrelevant to the lesson?

If someone asks about baptism at this stage, should the leader pursue that question? One among many may have a unique question that he may really be interested in. The others may not be all that interested in the question. The leader should not put the person down, but he can say something like this, "That is a good question, but if you don't mind, we will go ahead with our topic tonight and this question will be dealt with later." Usually this satisfies, but if the person is needing an answer, the leader can talk with him privately following the study, or at another time. Since this question may be out of context, it should not be dealt with in the group because it can cause confusion. It is not unusual to have questions that are of a philosophical and argumentative nature and the leader must not be pulled into this trap.

◆ **What if** the people are illiterate?

For this system of indirect leadership to work, you need at least one person who can read. (The leader could be that one.) If you have a group of twenty and only two can read, what do you do? Let one person read the question aloud and the other read the verse from the Bible. The ones who cannot read can give the answer. They have heard the question and the verse which contains the answer, so they can make the analysis and give the answer. While they will not be reading and writing, they will still be hearing, thinking, and analyzing, which is much better than listening to a sermon or lecture. The people hear, think, and decide.

◆ **What if** children come?

It will be a rare occasion when you do not have children in attendance. This can be handled in several ways.

One, if the children are quiet and sit with parents they will not interfere. Unless you have a team member to take care of the children, this may be the only option. I personally have never had a separate meeting for the children. Sometimes small children (under age ten) will tend to distract.

A second option will be to take workers to have "classes" for the children. These workers may come from a nearby church or be team members.

It will take time but it is often better to wait until leadership for children comes naturally from the group.

One thing for sure, the church planter cannot be oblivious to children and their needs. He must show real love and at the same time help the adults understand the Bible study material is for the mind of the adult.

◆ **What if** only children come?

Wait until adults come. If they do not come, go to another place where adults will attend. Remember the target is adults and your objective is church planting.

◆ **What if** only two or three adults come?

This depends on the culture and responsiveness to the Gospel. In some places two or three may be the most that could be hoped for. In that case the study would proceed with that number.

If you are using a cluster approach (dealt with in another chapter) three may be a good number since there may be many groups with this many or more.

If the study is in a responsive area where the cluster approach is not being used, I would be concerned about the small number and would postpone the study until more come. If more do not come, I would normally close out and go to a place where there is potential for a broader base upon which a church could be born. A close listening to the voice of the Holy Spirit is vital here.

LESSON TWO - third week

Begin with music

Review the songs learned at the last meeting. Often I will ask if anyone remembers one of the songs. If a hand goes up, I will ask that person to lead the song. Sometimes they will do it, but if they hesitate, I will ask them to come and assist me in leading the song. Involve the people every time possible. They are more willing and capable than we may think. After singing the songs of the previous week, I will introduce one or two more songs. There have been times I asked if there is someone who would like to sing a solo. It is not unusual for someone to come forward and sing one of the hymns which the group has just sung or even a secular song. This is no problem. Get the people involved.

Begin the lesson

Memory verse

I ask how many memorized the Scripture verse from last week's lesson. They are invited to stand and quote the verse. Some will do this every week and some will not. I do not put pressure here, since it might drive off the timid if they feel they may be called on to quote the verse publicly. The study of lesson two is led in the same way as the first lesson. This time the people are more comfortable and know how to participate. The lesson flows much more smoothly now. Let it flow from beginning to end without interruption and with little or no commentary. Let the Scripture speak.

Do not give an invitation after this lesson.

You may close the lesson with a question, "Do you have any questions about our lesson tonight?" Stay on target. Do not chase topics which would distract from the theme you want to plant deep in the minds of the people as they go home.

Give each one an appropriate tract.

What ifs...

◆ **What if** there are new members who missed the first week?

Do we help them catch up? How? This often is the week when there is the greatest turnover in attendance. Many of those who came for the first lesson may have come for reasons other than serious Bible study. Some may have come out of curiosity, and some to see what monetary gain there might be. When they see it is not entertainment and there are no opportunities for material gain, they drop out. But often new ones take their places.

If the turnover is up to fifty percent, I suggest you repeat the first lesson. You can face the problem with a positive ego-building statement like this: "As you can see, tonight we have many who missed out on the first lesson. Would you mind if we repeat the first lesson so these can catch up with you?" Those who finished the lesson will feel good about helping the others catch up, and the leader knows that repetition is the best thing in the world to help in learning. It does not hurt anyone; rather it helps.

Before beginning the lesson, take a moment to give some introductory remarks and introduce again how the lesson will be studied with everyone participating.

◆ **What if** there are two or three new ones who missed lesson one?

There are several ways this can be handled. One, the leader may make an appointment to meet with the new ones during the week and go through lesson one with them. This may be done individually or as a group.

Another way, which may be the best, is to ask one or two of the more enthusiastic and committed of the group to meet with the new members and help them go through lesson one before the next meeting time. This does two things, it boosts the confidence of the one helping; he learns that he can lead another through the lesson. Also, he learns more from doing it the second time with a friend than he did the first time in the group.

LESSON THREE - fourth week

Begin with music

Each week review the songs learned in previous weeks and introduce one or two new ones. If the people are eager to learn, they will be learning new songs every week outside the regular meeting times by using the cassette.

Begin the lesson

Memory verse - The members who memorized Romans 5:8 will stand and quote the verse.

By now the routine is familiar and the leader can sit, blend in with the group, and relax. He is in full control but keeps a low profile. He is doing something that should be reproducible in every aspect by anyone in the group.

Special music is not unusual by this time. Also various ones can now take turns in helping lead the group singing.

Close by asking the same question, "Do you have any questions about our lesson tonight?"

Give a tract to each one before they go home.

LESSON FOUR - fifth week

Begin with music

Follow the same pattern; expect wide participation by the members in the music leadership and special music. If there are instruments, let it be their instruments and their playing. If one of them can play a guitar, let him play if he desires. His playing is preferred, though it may be of less quality than that of the leader.

Memory verse - Members quote John 5:24

This lesson moves into the critical and crucial stage where the unbelievers begin to realize they are lost. Toward the end of the lesson I have heard spontaneous statements uttered sometimes in frustration, sometimes in anger, and sometimes in despair. Statements such as, "What must we do to be saved?" "Why didn't the church ever tell us about this?" "The church has lied to us all the time."

After having studied the lesson about Nicodemus and what it means to be born again, I close the lesson by reading the last question which asks, "Have you been born again?" It is amazing how one by one the members declare that they are not yet born again. By this time there is a rapport and trust built up between the leader and the members; they feel free to be open and honest.

To their acknowledgment that they have not been born again, I say, "Be sure to come back next week and we will look closer at what it means to born again."

I do not give an invitation at this point because I know the content of lessons five and six will provide a greater surety of genuine conversion.

At the close I give each one a tract.

What ifs...

◆ **What if** new people attend for the first time?

These should not be neglected. Having missed crucial lessons of the study, they are not ready to blend in where the group is. The leader can arrange a special time to meet with them to help them work through the lessons. Or, as suggested earlier, the leader may ask someone in the group to arrange a time to meet with these new enrollees to work through the lessons until they catch up with the group.

◆ **What if** someone wants to be saved?

The leader must be sensitive to the group and what they are feeling. There may be someone who has had a great deal of seed sown in his heart in the past and is ready to make a commitment. If there is a person in the group who acknowledges such a desire, the leader can deal with the person privately after the group has left or make an appointment for another time. It needs to be very clear that not giving a formal invitation does not mean that an invitation is not given.

LESSON FIVE - sixth week

Begin with music

It is not unusual for members to be leading the songs by this time. The leader does not appoint a song leader for the group or for the future church, but natural leaders will emerge if we permit.

Memory verse - The members stand and quote John 3:3,16.

The group is now becoming very sensitive because they are learning that, though they have been religious, they are lost. They learn that, though they may have been nominal Christians, they are not really Christians because they have not been born again. They are nearing a time of decision and discomfort is to be expected. It is not pleasant to learn that one has been mistaken all along. This is pre-repentance time.

An invitation is built into the conclusion of lesson five. Yet even at this point I do not normally give a formal invitation. I know what is coming in lesson six. I remember my objective—the birth of a living, vibrant church made up of people with new natures. If it is obvious that all of the group understands and is ready, there is no reason to delay. However, my experience has been that, although they are very close to a decision, they still need the further explanations found in lesson six.

After this lesson I give a tract with a more complete salvation message such as **Four Spiritual Laws** or **Purpose for Living.** (I do not use these tracts as a primary tool to lead someone to the Lord; rather they are used as a supplement.)

LESSON SIX - seventh week

Begin with music - led by members from the group.

Memory verse - Members quote John 1:12

This is the lesson when I expect all, or nearly all, of the members to accept Christ as their Savior. I change the approach in leadership a bit at this point. If the people have a small blackboard or whiteboard, I will use it to do my own Bridge of Life step by step as the members do theirs. (If there is no blackboard readily available I will take a small one with me.) The members continue to read the questions and the Scripture verses, as in the other lessons, but as I move with them through the Bridge of Life, I will make more comments and elaborate on what it means to repent and believe. It is not a lecture or sermon, only remarks to emphasize and clarify. I spend the most time explaining the words going over the cross—hear, believe, has eternal life. Special attention is given to the meaning of believe. **Believe** as it relates to trusting, dependence, reliance upon, surrender, is dealt with. On the blackboard I will make a list of some of the areas of life which will be affected when one believes—areas such as business, family, money, investments, pleasure, sex, etc. I explain that to believe means a willingness to surrender all of these areas to Christ as the Lord of them. After all of the picture has been filled in, I make a list at the center bottom of the page with these words which describe a person without Christ—hopeless, peaceless, purposeless, powerless, joyless. After the members pray a sinners prayer accepting Christ, I remind them of their past as portrayed by these words, but now it has changed. To signify the change, I erase the "less" after each word. Now, because of their faith in Christ, they have hope, peace, purpose, power, and joy. This rings a bell if they have really been saved.

Decision time

If the planter is not sure how to lead them to a decision, he may follow the built-in invitation at the end of the lesson. This is a very crucial time. To fail here is fatal—fatal for the person who is not saved and for the planting of a church.

With the passing of seven weeks since the planter has first met the people, a trusting friendship has been developed. The planter has been in the homes of the members; he knows something about their families, their background and needs.

When the Bridge of Life has been completed, the leader can straightforwardly ask the members if they are ready to accept Christ as their Savior. They will understand what is being said. They feel comfortable enough to respond honestly. I will stress the seriousness and the cost of following Christ before I ask them if they are ready to make the decision. One by one I will look them in the eye and ask them if they are ready. One by one they will say yes or give a nod of the head. Some may not be ready, and I will not put pressure on them to follow the others. If the group is large, I may ask those who want to follow Christ to come forward, indicating their desire to be saved. The leader will be sensitive to the leadership of the Holy Spirit in every detail of the invitation.

After those respond indicating their desire to be saved, I again explain the sinners prayer and how each one is to pray. If there is a line of people, I will start at one end and say, "We will begin with you. One by one each of you will pray a simple prayer from your heart. Each one will pray aloud." If you expect them to, they can and will pray such a prayer. It is healthy to allow them to overcome pride enough to admit aloud that they are sinners, helpless and hopeless. The leader may have to help get them started by saying a "sample" prayer, but it should be emphasized to them that it is not the leaders prayer that matters; they must pray their own prayer.

Following decision time

I will say to the group, "If you were sincere, and I believe you were, you now are God's children. You now have eternal life. You have been born again. Remember the verse that you have memorized, John 5:24." I will read that verse slowly to the new believers. They are reminded of the words, hear, believe, have, eternal life. They readily identify and know this is now describing them. Joy and peace begins to swell in their hearts. I will then turn to another verse which they have earlier memorized, John 3:16. After reading this verse, I remind them that because of God's love and mercy they now have eternal life. I ask, "If a friend gave you a gift, what would you say?" They will answer, "Thank you." I will say, "God has given you new life with peace, purpose and joy that will never end. What do you say to Him?" Again, they answer, "Thank you." It is explained that as a new, baby Christian, their first prayer will be one of thanksgiving. One by one each will pray aloud a prayer of thanksgiving. This is music to the ears of the church planter and, for sure, all the angels in God's Heaven. This is the first great step toward the planting of a church.

It is a joyous night. I greet each one. There is a new feeling of brotherhood.

A new factor now becomes a part of every meeting from this moment on; prayer now has meaning since the members know the Father.

Close

It is appropriate that the leader lead in the closing prayer, a simple prayer of thanksgiving. He will remember to model a short, reproducible prayer.

What ifs...

◆ **What if** some do not make a decision?

This is not unusual. For some reason, not understanding or simple rebellion, there may be a few who are not ready to make a decision. That is the reason for the simple seventh lesson which is designed to draw the net again.

◆ **What if** no one makes a decision?

Don't be discouraged. Lesson seven draws the net again.

LESSON SEVEN - eighth week

Begin with Prayer

Briefly explain what prayer is and how to pray. As leader, you may want to pray the first prayer. My prayer at this stage will be something like this, "Dear God, thank you for helping us be born again. Please guide our study tonight. Amen." Remember reproducibility. You are going to expect one of the members to close the meeting with prayer, so model a simple prayer that they can understand and reproduce.

Singing

At this stage, special music should be normal and the leadership of music should be out of the hands of the church planter.

Memory verse - Members will quote Ephesians 2:8-9

Lesson seven - the final net

This lesson reaffirms in the minds of the new believers their new standing with Christ. But the primary concern is for those few who may not have been ready to make a decision at the previous meeting. The method of study is the same as in the other lessons.

Invitation

The planter does not pull any punches, he goes for genuine decisions. He knows that this lesson ends the series designed to bring people to faith in Christ. He knows that from this point on there can be an evangelistic emphasis, but the main thrust must be feeding the new believers.

For those who respond and indicate they want to accept Christ, the leader should follow the same routine as he did in lesson six. Each one should be allowed to pray a prayer of acceptance and later pray a prayer of thanksgiving.

Seven lessons have been completed. Will the group continue? This depends entirely upon the group. I tell them this is the end of the study unless they want to continue. They are asked to make that decision. Normally they are eager to continue. They have found new life and are excited about their new relationship which has brought peace and joy.

I have experienced times when the group has decided not to continue. Usually this decision has been arrived at before the end of the lessons. The most common reason for stopping has been strong community pressure. On several occasions I have seen an entire community make a decision for the group. When all friends, family, and neighbors meet and say the group cannot continue, there is not much hope in the immediate future for the group.

What ifs...

◆ **What if** there are some who still have not made a decision to accept Christ?

Much depends on whether the group continues to meet. If they decide not to continue beyond lesson seven, it may mean a closed door for further witnessing.

If the group continues to meet and the unbelievers still come, the planter will need to give them personal attention outside the meeting time. From this point the main emphasis of the studies needs to be the feeding of the new believers.

◆ **What if** only a few from the group have been saved?

The leader has two options. One is to shake the dust off and move on to another place. The other is, if the group wants to continue, the planter will continue a study of portions of the Bible that deal with salvation. He may choose to do a case study of Biblical characters who were saved.

◆ **What if** the group is forced to stop meeting?

There is not much the planter can do. He cannot force the issue; it would only create greater problems for the new believers and close the door tighter for further ministry. The church planter is not defeated. Souls have been saved. Some will be in heaven someday because of the study. The future climate may change so he can go back in for follow-up.

◆ **What if** the group wants to continue?

This is the normal response. The new believers enthusiastically express a desire to continue. The Church planter should have a copy of *I Have Been Born Again, What Next?* with him when the seventh lesson is finished. As soon as the group expresses a desire to continue, he will show them this book and suggest they use it for the next study.

SECTION IV

THE BIRTH OF A CHURCH

Chapter 22

They Have Been Born Again, What Next?

(Second step toward the birth of the church—orientation)

The first step was the salvation of individuals in the group. Now that they have been saved, it is logical for them to be asking, "Now what?" *I Have Been Born Again, What Next?* has been designed in the midst of church planting to answer this question. It takes the people where they are and leads them to a basic understanding of discipleship and responsible church membership.

Introduction to *I Have Been Born Again, What Next?*

There are eleven lessons which will require about one hour each. The lessons are progressive, taking the new believer from where he is, to the point of baptism and church membership. I feel it is best to follow the lessons in the order given. Someone may have a question about a subject such as baptism immediately after they are saved. But the group is not likely to be asking that question. The lessons before baptism deal with the questions logically faced by most new believers. If one person should want to study baptism before there is a study of the other topics, I would normally suggest that this is a good question, but if he doesn't mind we will deal with that topic a little later. The leader must be aware of the very vocal people. He should not assume the group is at the same place as the one person who may ask any question that pops into his mind. This person should not be allowed to determine the direction of the study for the entire group. The church planter should be more aware of what the people need than they are. After leading many groups from the point of salvation to becoming a church, I am convinced the following sequence of topics meets most of the real needs of the new converts.

The titles of the lessons are:

1. **A New Nature**

2. **A New Power: The Holy Spirit**

3. **A New Guide: Bible Study**

4. **A New Privilege: Prayer**

5. **A New Hope**

6. **New Relationships**

7. **A New Understanding of Baptism**

8. **A New Family: The Church**

9. **A New Reminder: The Lord's Supper**

10. **A New Opportunity: Tithing**

11. **A New Responsibility**

Each member should have his personal copy of this book.

Good News For You and the **Gospel of John** are provided free of cost, but now that the members have new life and new motives, they should be permitted to purchase *I Have Been Born Again, What Next?* In many languages it is available at a reasonable price, therefore affordable for the people. (There may be cases where the church planter will need to subsidize the cost of these books, but should not pay the full amount.)

FIRST WEEK IN THE NEW STUDY

Meeting place

It is likely the group will continue to meet at the same time and place as the previous eight weeks. This is the decision of the group, not of the church planter.

The meeting will last for about one hour and may follow the procedure used in the *Good News For You* study.

Open with **prayer**

Expect someone from the group to lead in prayer, even if it is one sentence. The planter may have to review for a moment the meaning of prayer and how to pray.

Group **singing**

This will continue just as in the past few weeks. Someone from the group will lead the singing. Special music will come from the group. There is no need for a complicated music program.

Study of Chapter One in *I Have Been Born Again, What Next?*

The church planter may want to guide the study of this chapter as a role model and expect someone from the group to lead the second lesson. Clear instructions are given in the front of the book, but the planter should briefly share that he will guide the group as they participate in the study. If the group is large, each one may read a paragraph or two. Let everyone have a turn in reading. Let it flow without interruption. The leader should not expound at every point. The lessons are programmed to answer questions that need to be answered.

Remember reproducibility. If the leader is too talkative, don't expect someone from the group to feel comfortable leading the study next week.

Why not ask the members to take the book home and read the chapter, then let the leader lecture on the topic? In some places this may work, but in my experience, most of the them will not do their homework.

After the members have read the lesson aloud, they will continue by reading and answering the questions at the end of the chapter.

This can be a very interesting time. The members feel somewhat relaxed and free to be themselves. In a study I was leading, members were sharing about how their lives had changed since they were born again. The Japanese lady to my right said, "I am more aware of when I sin now than before." A young man said, "It is not nearly as easy for women to seduce me as it was before." Another said, "I don't drink like I did." It is a thrill to observe a group who has been inhabited by the Holy Spirit.

At the conclusion of the lesson the leader may ask if there are any questions on the lesson. Usually there are none.

The leader asks one of the members to guide the study of chapter two. He may need to explain that the member is to do just what he has done on lesson one.

Someone from the group will lead in closing prayer.

The study of the next ten lessons will follow the same pattern as lesson one. The leader may ask a different one to lead the lesson each week. There have been times when I have guided all of the lessons, but feel it is usually best to allow members to participate whenever possible, and it is possible for them to guide these studies. The church planter will be present and retain leadership of the group, but he may sit and say very little during the entire lesson.

It is important that all the members have the opportunity to lead in public prayer during the weeks of this study. Assume they will, and they will—if the leader models properly and expects the maximum from the believers.

Chapter 23

Second Objective Reached: The Birth of a Church

By the time the group has been together for eight weeks for the pre-salvation stage and for another eleven weeks for the pre-church stage, they are blending as a group with extraordinary relationships. Normally, by the end of the study of *I Have Been Born Again, What Next?* they understand enough to be ready to become a church.

When does a group become a church? In the Ephesians sense of the Body of Christ, the group becomes a church when they become a part of God's family through the new birth. When a group of people accept Christ and there is a total change in attitudes and relationships, there is a very real sense in which the family relationship emerges. There is a feeling of brotherhood long before the baptismal service. The group becomes a church in the local sense when they are baptized. In this baptism there is a double identification, the public identification as followers of Christ and the public announcement that they are a new church.

The church planter can assume they will continue as a new church. I have never asked them if they want to become a church. To ask them that is like asking a fish if it wants to swim. It is natural for them to desire this and the study has prepared them for this step.

The church planter will ask about the best date for the baptism, then review what it means to be baptized and become a church.

If the planter is the only baptized believer in the group, there is no question about who will do the baptizing.

The planter may desire to issue baptismal certificates.

When a group is baptized, they become a full-fledged church. They are not a house church, store church, market church, or mission point. They are as much a church as they will ever be. There will be development, new programs, new buildings, etc., but they do not have to wait for all these to consider themselves a church. They do not even have to wait for a "constitution service," nor do they have to wait for neighboring churches to declare that they are a church. All of these may have their place, but a church they do not make.

SECTION V

POST BIRTH

Chapter 24

After the Birth: Development

The work of the church planter does not end with the birth of the church. Someone, either the planter, an associate who specializes in church development, or some other team member, must take seriously the training of leadership. On some occasions, the planter will become the pastor. This is not a problem if his goal is to plant only one church. If, however, his goal is to plant several churches, local leaders should be trained to pastor the churches. For the foreign missionary church planter, it is much better to train local leaders to be the pastors. Transferring leadership early allows the planter to plant many more churches. One basic principle I believe to be true is, the longer the foreign missionary holds on to the leadership responsibilities, the more difficult it is to transfer the leadership to a national. This is true in small churches, and from a study of twelve large city churches, I have found it is just as true for the "mega church." In this chapter we will assume the planter is a full time church planter who wants to plant many churches.

What does the church planter do after the baptism?

He may want to call a special meeting on the same day of the baptism to give the certificates of baptism and discuss the future.

The group will discuss the best **day for the regular worship service.** This usually will be Sunday, but this is for the members to decide. If they want to meet on another day, this is up to them. The planter will not dictate this, but may gently suggest Sunday. The **time** must be set for regular meetings. It would be a glimmer of paternalism if the foreign church planter told the people they should meet on Sunday morning with Sunday School at 9:00 and worship at 10:00. One new church in my church planting experience felt they should come together every night to discuss what God had done in their lives that day. They shared, sang and prayed on nights that were not "prayer meeting" night. They came together on Sunday morning at eight or nine o'clock and continued to meet until after noon. It was a strange setting for a traditional clock-watching westerner, but I wasn't about to tell them this was not the way other churches did it.

The group will need to discuss the following items.

Who will lead the worship service?

The group has the Holy Spirit leading them and it is amazing how well He can do it. It is true the new believers do not have much experience, but the Holy Spirit has adequate experience and wisdom. There will be times when the inexperienced new believers will obviously move in the wrong direction and the planter must gently keep them on track.

Who will lead the singing?

This is not a big problem. If the system I have shared has been followed, this part of the worship will come quite naturally with little change from what they have been doing. The members have been in charge of the music for several weeks. The natural song leader probably will have emerged by this time. Sometimes there are two or three who share in the music ministry and take turns leading the singing.

Who will lead in public praying?

There is no problem at this point since members have been doing this every week. There is no need for the church planter to do this except as one of the group.

Who will preach?

Perhaps at this point no one will "preach." Sometimes experienced church-goers think in terms of only one way, one approach to proclaiming the Biblical message. This is a man standing in the pulpit preaching a formal sermon. Effective worship is possible without the traditional sermon. The Word of God must not be neglected or minimized, but the communication of it will be within the Christ-sustained capability of the new believers. A pastor will not be named at this point. A regular preacher will not be appointed. In time this will likely happen, but now is too early. In Paul's writings to Timothy, he warned against the premature assignment of a man to the pastoral position.

Most small churches cannot afford to hire a full-time pastor, nor do they need one. This is especially true if the church starts with fifteen or twenty members. If the small, new church feels it must follow the pattern of the typical large, older church and have a full time professionally-trained pastor, the church is not likely to be self-supporting. Most new churches do not have the financial resources at the time of birth to employ a professional full-time pastor.

It should be noted that Paul himseif began preaching almost immediately following his conversion. The same chapter of Acts which tells of his conversion and baptism also tells of him "immediately" preaching. It is Biblical and currently possible for a man to preach immediately after he has been saved.

What is the church to do about choosing who will lead the worship service? The members know the more mature ones in the group and those who are more capable, respected, and responsible enough to lead the worship. They will chose from these. In the beginning, I think it is better to have a shared leadership in worship. It is easy to lock in on someone early before he has proven himself or had a chance to know if God is calling him, but it is difficult to remove that person if he is not the right one. Also, it just is not fair to the person to be put in such a strained position.

For the next Sunday the group will select someone to guide the worship service. There will be no significant change in the order of service as followed for the eleven weeks study of *I Have Been Born Again, What Next?* The singing will continue; the praying will continue; there will be special music. The only difference is in the kind of study. There will be a change in content; the study will focus sharply on the Bible.

We all know you cannot normally expect a new believer to preach a sermon the Sunday following his baptism. I have prepared a book to be used in this exact situation. It is entitled **Galatians, From Law to Grace**. With a few minutes of instruction from the planter, the leader for the next Sunday can easily use this book to lead the worship service. We must remember that a climate has been established which allows the members to feel that all are ministers with responsibilities to the body and to the world. It is never intended to be a one-man show, so they do not expect anything except group worship and feeding from the Word. Neither showmanship nor dictatorship have been a part of their new life.

The leader can use the Galatians study guide for a group-participation style of worship, or he may use it as his guide for a lecture/sermon presentation. If he chooses to use it for group participation, it is best if each member has a copy of the guide. But if they do not, the leader can permit the members to take turns reading portions from the Bible chapter and he can read the commentary from the guide. **It should be stressed that the Bible is the text of authority**, thus the Scripture should be read first and then the commentary. Each chapter of Galatians is outlined. At the end of each chapter there is a section for discussion and review. The members should participate in this. With the music and one chapter, not much more than one hour is needed. The study of Galatians will take six weeks.

Note the rationale for the study of Galatians at this point. The theme of the book makes it very relevant, since most people come out of a works-oriented concept of salvation. Galatians reaffirms that their salvation is by grace and not by law or works.

How can we teach new believers to feed daily on the Word?

For wholeness of life, both physical and spiritual, Jesus stated the absolute necessity for the Word in the life of God's people. *But Jesus answered, "The scripture says, 'Man cannot live on bread alone, but needs every word that God speaks.'"* Matthew 4:4

Churches are often planted with the vague hope that the members will study the Bible. The traditional Sunday School will not get the job done. It will supplement, but if it is the primary tool to get believers into the Word, we are in a sad situation. This is where we are today in the United States and around the world where we have transferred our western programs, thinking they will automatically work in every land. The traditional Sunday School is on the decline around the world.

How can we change this situation? First, we must expect more from believers. In addition to the regular worship service, I have assumed the new church will have a time where Bible reading and study can be emphasized. This could be called the Sunday School, but I am talking about something much different from a traditional Sunday School lesson with some Scripture and a lot of commentary which often is not relevant to the lives of the new believers. The new church needs to immediately get into serious exposure to the Word in a manner which will minister to their current spiritual needs.

On more than one occasion I have heard missionaries who have been driven out of countries by communism tell how they left so much with the believers, organizations, institutions, buildings, etc., but the greatest regret was the failure to leave the people in the Word. There is nothing more significant in the planting of a church than being sure that the believers are daily feeding on the Word. The problems of leadership development begin to fade when the whole church is involved in feasting on the Word. Jumping from place to place in the Bible doing our "daily Bible readings" will not get the job done. This may be enough to inoculate against guilt, but not enough to set a church on fire for God. Give me a church whose every member is prayerfully reading through the Bible every year and you can have all the other training programs. Degrees from seminaries will not be as beneficial as a lifetime of repeatedly reading through the Bible.

How do we get a new church into God's Word? There are many ways, but let me suggest a simple way which can be easily implemented by any church, even without special leadership training. No special books are needed, only the Bible. Encourage the believers to own a Bible in a modern translation. It is important that the new believers understand the language of the Bible they read.

First, church planters and leaders must be setting an example that reveals a regular, fruitful, and joyful Bible reading program. Anyone who believes the Bible to be the Word of God will find excitement and challenge when reading it. This excitement will be contagious. Church members will be aware of it.

Even though the members may be challenged to begin a Bible reading program, they need something to help them remain faithful. It is natural for a person to excitedly begin something, but after a while lose the excitement. It is often like this with Bible reading. **Accountability** is important in all a person does. Our course of action is usually influenced when we are accountable to someone.

Bible reading report time

This is a time when the members are accountable to the group for their Bible reading. The size of the church will make a difference in how this is done. A small church may have Bible reading report time before the worship hour, either on Sunday morning or Sunday night. Some may prefer another special time for this. If the church is large, it may be necessary to divide into small groups. An hour or more could be used in this time of sharing.

It should be assumed that every member will be involved in daily Bible reading. Therefore, every member should be expected to participate in the report time. This is not a time of preaching, lecturing, or sharing ones own ideas. It is a time to share directly from the Bible great verses that have spoken to the person that week. In the appendix you will find a sample Calendar for Personal Bible Reading which members may use to keep record of their Bible reading. A diary, any calendar, or a small notebook could be used.

The Bible reading report time is more than a system of accountability. It is more than checking up on each other; it is a sharing with others. It is a method of teaching each other. The Bible has something to say about the Word being used by all to teach each other. Romans 15:14 says *My brothers: I myself feel sure that you are full of goodness, that you are able to teach one another.* In I Corinthians 14:31 Paul says, *All of you may proclaim God's message, one by one, so that everyone will learn and be encouraged.*

Some may ask, "Isn't it boring to do this, just to read the Bible?" It depends on what a person thinks of God's Word. For His child, it should never be boring. What God's Word says is much more exciting and important than what any person says about God's Word. Paul said, *Until I come, give your time and effort to the public reading of the Scriptures and to preaching and teaching.* 1 Timothy 4:13 Note that Paul speaks of three activities, public reading, preaching, and teaching.

In the Old Testament we read about Ezra reading the Word of God to the people. *So Ezra brought it to the place where the people had gathered—men, women, and the children who were old enough to understand. There in the square by the gate he read the Law to them from dawn until noon, and they all listened attentively. . . .When the people heard what the Law required, they were so moved that they began to cry. . . . So all the people went home and ate and drank joyfully and shared what they had with others, because they understood what had been read to them.* Nehemiah 8:2-3,9,12 Of another occasion we read, *for about three hours the Law of the Lord their God was read to them, and for the next three hours they confessed their sins and worshipped the Lord their God.* Nehemiah 9:3 Joshua was very direct when he said, *Be sure that the book of he Law is always read in your worship. Study it day and night, and make sure that you obey everything written in it.* Joshua 1:8

There is nothing more important to the health of the church than for each church member to stay faithfully in the Word of God. The Holy Spirit will be the teacher and guide as the believer reads and studies. Of all books, the Bible is **The Book**. Those who read it will be changed. Like the Shepherd of Psalm 23, it is the church leader's responsibility to lead "his people" to rest in fields of green grass and to lead them to quiet pools of fresh water. It is the Word that nourishes and refreshes the believer.

What does the new leader use after he has led the congregation through the six chapters of Galatians?

If he is a new convert, it is unlikely the leader will be ready, even with weekly training, to prepare and preach Bible-based sermons each week. I have prepared a study guide to be used with the Gospel of John to meet this need. The study with *John; Behold the Lamb* will be a little different than the Galatians study. The format is more of an expository treatment of Scripture. It is a chapter-by-chapter study of John and will provide 21 weeks of study. It is designed to do two things: First, to keep the leader in the Scripture and second, to teach him how to prepare expository sermons. The leader may choose to use this as a guide in his preparation, using it as a springboard. Or he may choose to use it in a similar way as he used Galatians, having group participation with various members taking turns reading, first the Scripture and then the commentary on that portion.

The rationale for using John's Gospel at this point: The new converts need an emphasis on the deity of Christ and His work. John also gives a refreshing view of how a person is saved. The new converts need this review and emphasis.

Following twenty-one weeks in John, *Romans: The Road to Righteousness* can be used. This study guide is much like the one on John. It is a chapter-by-chapter expository treatment of the sixteen chapters in Romans. The leader may follow it very closely or he may use it only as a guide.

The rationale for using Romans at this point: Romans is a blown up, enlarged picture of Galatians. New converts need to be exposed to this wide range of theological issues.

By the time the leader has taken the congregation through these three books, he will be better equipped to continue feeding the believers from the Word. Of course, **we assume additional pastoral leadership training to be ongoing immediately following the birth of the church.**

Chapter 25

Leadership Training

Leadership training begins before the church is born. As the planter involves participants in the Bible study he is training leaders. Through their participation and his example, training is going on all the time. His influence is felt before a training class is scheduled. For a moment let us take note of the church planter's influence on new believers and future leaders.

The influence of the Bible study leader on the life of the new believer is tremendous—sometimes negative, but hopefully most often positive.

There is the incarnate, caught more than taught, influence. This is the unstructured influence which comes through being, in contrast to structured, planned influence. This is the "candid camera" influence wherein the Bible study leader, attitudes and actions being observed, becomes a model for the new believers. Love, humility, and urgent concern are seen in the daily life of the leader and are "caught" by the new believers.

In the beginning, the most powerful model influencing the new believer is not the written Word, the Bible, but the incarnate word as modeled by the Bible study leader. The first principles of godly living are seen in the life-style of the leader, the church planter. The new believer, so in need of positive influence and nurture, sees the model—the Bible study leader, before he has an opportunity to explore the Bible in depth.

Every attitude, every action of the leader is important because, conscious of it or not, young spiritual eyes are looking, learning, and being influenced. The leader is a powerful model, constantly displaying attitudes, theology, and methodology.

The planter is soon aware that new believers are great imitators, and in time, the leader sees himself mirrored in the lives of those under his influence.

While most of the leader's influence is caught through life-style modeling, he also influences new believers as they are taught in structured teaching situations. A serious leader realizes that a complete reprogramming of the new believer's mind is the Biblical standard set by Christ. The reprogramming begins with a total new mind- and heart-set toward God. Then, following the Biblical pattern, new attitudes evolve relating to fellowmen, and new social dimensions arise. The Bible study leader understands that Paul's mandate, *Let this mind be in you, which was also in Christ Jesus*, (Philippians 2:5 KJV) becomes the goal toward which he will influence the new believers with whom he works.

Through lessons both caught and taught, the Bible study leader conveys a standard of expectation to the new believers. There is a danger of negative influence when a leader ministers to people who have less education (Biblical or otherwise) or who have fewer financial advantages than himself. A silent sense of superiority tends to seep through. This superior feeling on the part of the Bible study leader can result in a debilitating paternalism which blinds the leader to the dignity and potential of the new believer. The leader's expectations will be overshadowed with assumptions that, "They can't . . .," "They cannot afford . . .," "They are not able . . .," etc. Usually, the new believer concurs that the leader is right. "We can't" then becomes the mind-set of the new believers, causing them to always need the crutch of an outsider. Dependency is bred and a retarded believer is born.

The Bible study leader influences all the future of the new believer when he sets standards of expectation of dignity, freedom, and unlimited potential, with God as the source. The leader serves as the earliest standard of expectation because the new believer knows the leader better than he knows the Bible. The level of expectation is firmly set in the early days of the Christian life. The leader must believe, must expect, that the new believer, with God's help, can become and do all the leader is and does. This should be expected to be the norm for the believer. If this norm is not realized, it is probably because the leader does not expect it. We may call this the power of positive expectation. The planter's influence hinges greatly upon his low or high level of expectation.

When the magnitude of this influence is rightly understood by the leader, in trembling awe, he bows before God, constantly needing and seeking wisdom. To be a part of a holy triangle composed of the Holy Spirit and the Bible study leader, touching, shaping, and reprogramming the minds of others, is an awesome responsibility.

As a tiny pebble tossed into a calm pool of water sends ripples far beyond itself and its immediate presence, so one new, revolutionized life sends ripples through society. When a church planter realizes this powerful influence, he will want to toss as many pebbles as possible, thus bringing Christ to a family, a community, a town, a province, even a nation, and unto the uttermost places.

So this is leadership training, even before a class is taught or a school is entered. From the beginning and on through formal training, the model set by the initial leader, the church planter, and his expectation level is very important. His "followers" will rise as high as he expects and seldom higher.

FORMAL LEADERSHIP TRAINING

Immediately following the baptismal service and before the first worship service, someone should begin a scheduled class for leadership training. The trainer may be the church planter or a member of a church planting team. It is very logical and natural for the person who has been working with the group from the beginning to help them in the elementary stages of leadership training. He knows where they are and what they need. If the trainer is someone other than the church planter, that person should be exposed to the way the church was born and all that has transpired in the previous four months. He also must follow the same principles of church growth as practiced by the church planter if there is to be harmonious growth. Normally, the church planter is in the best position to lead the basic training.

Who may attend the leadership training class?

At this early stage I prefer to open it up to anyone who wants to attend. I do not know all those who have the potential to become leaders. I have had classes with as many as eight when the beginning membership of the new church totaled twenty-six. At that particular church this was not a problem. After a few weeks those with adequate interest continued and the others dropped out.

What do they need to study?

If the church planting has been done among unbelievers, the training must be very basic. Nothing should be assumed.

Some of the areas of study will include:

- The Bible, and its makeup
- The worship service

- The call from God to be a pastor
- Qualifications for a pastor
- The work of a pastor
- Sermon preparation
- How to witness
- Basic doctrines
- Church officers
- How to lead a group Bible study
- How to start a new church

The primary book I have used in leadership training is the Bible. Within its pages one will find all that is necessary to equip a person to be an effective minister, whether it be the ministry of pastoring or any other ministry. There are some supplementary books which I have found to be helpful. The primary one I use, *Questions People and Churches Ask,* has been written to meet fundamental needs in the early days of leadership training. It has fifty-two questions most often asked by new believers and new churches. I will not go straight through the book; rather as needs arise, the group will study the chapters that apply. Before the next baptismal service after the birth of the church, the group in leadership training class will study the chapters about the meaning of Christian baptism and how to administer baptism.

The value of the book, *Questions People and Churches Ask,* is its simplicity in meeting needs of the people where they are in their Christian growth, with the Bible as the authority.

Three other major books which come after the basics have been studied are: *Let This Mind Be in You,* by Brock, *A Quest for Vitality in Religion,* by Findley Edge, *The Company of the Committed,* by Elton Trueblood. These three books strongly reinforce what I have sought to emphasize from the birth of the church.

The leadership class is customized to meet the needs of the group. There may be one or there may be ten in the class. The class will continue weekly for many months. After several churches have been born in the general area, it is possible to continue a central training class with leaders coming from different churches. The need for training will not end. If the church planter is fortunate, there will be a local Bible school or seminary extension classes where the leaders can enroll for further training.

In many countries a planter must be aware of what may happen if new leaders go far away to receive theological education. There are some inherent dangers, one of which is the leader may never be able to come back down to the level of the people to be able to effectively minister to them. There is also the danger of reason replacing faith as the student preacher moves to a more purely intellectual approach to the Bible. A serious planter wants men trained to proclaim the Word without trying to decide what part of it is God's Word. As one promising young graduate said to me on his graduation day, "Before I came here three years ago, my shirt was wet when I finished preaching, now when I preach it is always dry." In many parts of the world the logical step in indigenous growth is for a local Bible school to eventually evolve, sponsored and directed by the local churches.

Chapter 26

Church Organizational Meeting

Within a week or two following the baptismal service and birth of the church, it is usually necessary to have a meeting where some formal planning and organization is done. The church planter should lead this meeting.

In *I Have Been Born Again, What Next?* the members have already studied about the need for and the qualifications of a church secretary and treasurer. It will be helpful to review these positions. After a clear understanding, the members will choose individuals to fill these positions. It is usually best to formally elect the ones leading the music. It is good to have an assistant to the treasurer. The group will decide which bank to use and how to open up the account. Every withdrawal should require the signature of the treasurer and the assistant treasurer. In third world nations, the use and misuse of church money can be a major problem. A monthly reporting system must be instituted if people are expected to continue giving.

After a few months, it may be helpful for the church to consider writing up and adopting a constitution and by-laws.

Should the church planter attend all of the worship services of the new church?

It depends on his schedule. Many full-time church planters will be planting more than one church at a time. If this is the first church he has planted, he will have more free time on Sundays. There is no problem for him to attend as often as possible, as long as he can relax and let the new believers lead. If he thinks he must have a say on everything they do or do everything for them, he becomes their greatest deterrent to growth. If he can go to a worship service and sit among the people as one of them without being called on to do anything, he should feel good. Only those who are secure and confident will be comfortable in doing this.

The planter goes primarily as an encourager, not as a supervisor. As his responsibilities grow with the birth of more churches, he will be able to visit each church less frequently and this is good. He will be respected and loved by the new believers as long as he lives.

Chapter 27

The Church Receiving New Members

Churches tend to be weak and compromising at this point. Some fear being too demanding; others may be unaware of the eternal consequences of a membership made up of both believers and unbelievers. Nothing will dilute the witness of a church as much as having a membership of world-styled members. Therefore, when a new church is born, the reception of new members is critical.

Historical track records leave much to be desired. Even in older churches in the Bible belt of the United States, serious new member orientation is almost nonexistent. In one large city of the south I made a study of thirty-one churches. Some of these are very large and very "successful." Only one had anything that resembled a serious orientation for new members. For many it was like this: After a sermon, a new-member applicant would walk down the isle and share with the pastor or another leader his desire to join the church either by baptism or transfer of membership from another church of similar faith. Orientation for the new member would consist of a tour of the building, an introduction to staff members and, maybe, a brief introduction to some of the church programs. Some churches have orientation programs which can be carried out in one hour. The majority simply invite the new member to attend the appropriate Sunday School class. From that point on, he is on his own to sink or swim. Some churches make new-member orientation materials available and may even have a class for new members, but it is highly optional. Membership tends to be easy and undemanding.

Generally, if a new member is a transferee from another church, it would be unthinkable to assume that he give his personal testimony before being accepted for membership. As a pastor I found myself in this rut, a common rut for most churches I knew about. Little was expected of new members. If they wanted to attend worship or didn't want to that was not a serious problem. They were accepted without a sign of a changed life. The church of which I was pastor was doing a special study of *A Quest for Vitality in Religion* by Findley Edge. The study was causing the members to think about authentic faith and a regenerate church membership. One Sunday morning we had a fine crowd at the worship service. A family of five was visiting our church looking for a new church home where they could serve. After the sermon, I gave a traditional invitation. A woman with the appearance of a disco dancer, came to the front. As usual with those making decisions, I asked some very simple questions. This particular woman came for membership from another church of like faith from another state. As a good, normal pastor, I asked her to stand with me at the front as I introduced her and shared with the congregation the nature of her decision. I said, "She comes requesting membership based on transfer of letter from _____ Church. All of you who welcome her into our church, please make it known by an uplifted hand."

After the closing prayer I met this fine family who was searching for a church home. He asked, "Did you know that woman who joined your church this morning?" Normally, I had previous knowledge of those making decisions such as this, but I had never seen this woman before. I could only say, "No, I never knew her before today." The man said, "Now she is a member of your church, isn't she?" Again, I could only say, "Yes, she is." His response was, "Well, if being a member of your church means no more than that, we will have to look somewhere else." Later in the day he called me at home, saying I should look in the newspaper to see a picture of our new member. She was an entertainer at a local night club.

Our church had to rethink the way members were received. We had to rethink our responsibility to properly orient new members. A major change was experienced. From that point on, potential new members could present themselves for membership just as before, but they were accepted only as candidates for membership. They were not presented for membership until we had heard about their conversion experiences and were sure they knew about the privileges and responsibilities of being church members. If a candidate was not serious, he would not be accepted. He had to be serious enough to attend regular church services. His lifestyle must be that of a believer. We owe it to the church body and to the candidate to take membership more seriously.

The problem today in our churches is not so much a "back door problem" as it is a "front door problem." The time to deal with this problem is at the birth of a new church. Deal with it before the fresh, invigorating, demanding standards of expectation begin to fall. This is one of the many joys of a church planter.

Note some simple suggestions on receiving new members.

New members are usually added by baptism or by transfer from another church of the same faith and practice. We will look at both of these.

RECEIVING NEW MEMBERS BY BAPTISM

The following steps are suggested.

1. Proper counseling is done to be as sure as possible the person is really born again and has a new lifestyle.

2. The person comes before the church during the worship service, stating that he has been born again and desires to be baptized and be a member of the church.

3. The church recognizes the person as a candidate for baptism and membership.

4. The candidate must be willing and able to give a clear testimony of his salvation experience. He will be given an outline to help him in writing out his testimony. (A copy of an outline is found in the appendix of this book.) A church leader may need to help in the preparation of both the written and oral testimony. The written testimony is assuming the literacy of the candidate. In case of illiteracy, an oral testimony will suffice.

5. Before the next worship service, the candidate should submit the written testimony to the church leader or some other designated person.

6. At a following worship or special service the candidate will give his testimony, telling in detail about how, where, and when he was born again.

7. The candidate then attends a new member class for a prescribed period. If *I Have Been Born Again, What Next?* is used for new member orientation, the sessions will last for eleven weeks. The candidate must complete this orientation study or another which the church may decide to use. A customized study may take less time. For some, it may be better to do the lessons on their own at home. A designated church leader could meet with the candidate at certain intervals to answer questions and discuss those things the candidate has studied.

The new member class can be held at any time convenient to the candidates for membership. The church will elect the leaders of the new member orientation class. (If the church has additions on a regular basis, it may be helpful to have more than one new member class.)

8. During the course of orientation study, the church will have opportunity to observe the behavior of the candidate. Not only will his moral behavior be observed, but also his faithful attendance in the activities of the church.

9. After the candidate has completed the orientation and has proven he is really interested in being a part of the church family, his name will be presented to the church at a regular monthly business meeting.

If the candidate has not been willing to give his testimony or fulfill the requirements for new-member orientation, he should not be presented to the church for acceptance. The leader should report on the candidate but postpone acceptance until the candidate shows that he is serious enough to comply with the requirements for membership.

If the candidate has met the requirements and has shown a faithful spirit of participation in worship, the church leader will recommend to the church that the candidate be accepted for baptism and full church membership.

10. The church will vote to receive the person for baptism and membership.

11. When the candidate is baptized, he becomes a member of the church.

RECEIVING NEW MEMBERS BY STATEMENT OR TRANSFER

Repeat all of the above steps except #10 and #11. Number ten is changed to read: The church will vote to receive the person for membership.

Members added by statement or transfer are people who are already baptized members of another church of the same faith and practice. It is important that the church a prospective member comes from has the same basic doctrines and practices as the church he is seeking to join. If he comes in with different doctrines, the result will be disunity within the church family and this cannot be allowed.

The church secretary should obtain the name and address where the candidate is a member and write to the church requesting information about the person. It should be asked if he is a member of the church and if he is in good standing. When the new candidate is received into the church family as a member, the secretary then should write another letter to that church telling them that this particular person has joined this church. (This allows the other church to drop the person's name from their list of members.)

A healthy church must be strong and strict at the point of orientation and acceptance of new members. It is not a matter of sitting in critical "judgment;" rather it is recognizing as important the witness of the local church and the importance of having responsible members.

Chapter 28

How Does a Church Get a Pastor?

Several factors influence a church getting a pastor.

- The size of the congregation
- The needs of the congregation
- The financial strength of the congregation
- The age of the church
- The availability of pastoral leadership outside the congregation

It is wrong to assume that a church must get a pastor from outside the congregation. God can, and often does, call men from the membership of the church to serve as pastors/leaders.

We will look at two common situations when churches need to get pastors. At all times the Holy Spirit should guide the church in the matter of calling a man to be their pastor.

1. How does the new church with a small membership and limited financial resources get a pastor?

After the birth of the church, the members may ask one or more of the men to alternate leading the worship services. These men will preach/teach/lead. There will be a need for weekly leadership training classes. The classes will be very basic, dealing with the very practical aspects of pastoral work. Emphasis will be put on how to prepare a sermon and how to do other pastoral duties. It needs to be pointed out that the western style of worship is not always needed nor even best, especially when a church is young with leaders of little experience. A song service led by a member, followed with the reading and discussion of a chapter from the Bible, may be just as effective as the traditional three songs and a sermon. Both may be effective. Wide participation by the members is very desirable. The same person should not lead the singing, play the guitar, pray, teach, and preach.

Normally at this early stage the worship leader should not be thought of as the pastor. It may be a while before the leaders and the church members are sure who has been given the gift of pastoring. But in time, all will know. If five men start out rotating as worship leaders, after a few months this number may be down to two. Both of these may end up being regular leaders. Usually it will be best for one to be recognized as pastor and the other as associate pastor. There is strength in having two or more such leaders sharing the preaching, especially if they are bivocational. (By bivocational we mean that they may continue to make their living with another job and at the same time serve the church.) The burden is lighter when two or more share in the responsibilities. For a new Christian with little training, to be preparing one or two new sermons every week can become too heavy and he may become discouraged under the work load.

Often within a year after the birth of the church, the position of pastor/leader is settled.

Even though these men may be making a living with other employment, the church should begin as soon as possible giving a weekly love gift to the pastor/leader. As the church grows, the amount of this love gift should also grow. Any church related expenses, such as attending learning seminars, special classes, study materials, and travel expenses, should be paid by the church. These men are no less pastors than highly trained men serving full time in large churches.

As the church grows in number and financial ability to pay a full salary, it may be best to think of looking for someone to be a full-time pastor. It is possible that the person serving as part-time pastor may terminate his other employment and begin serving as full-time pastor. Through personal study the bivocational pastor may become as well trained as a man who has completed Bible school or seminary. But the church may desire to look outside the local church for a pastor who has more training.

2. How does the more financially able church find a pastor?

After much prayer, the congregation comes to a common agreement that a full-time pastor is needed, and that through the tithes and offering of the members, a full-time salary can be paid. (If the pastor is to be under the direction of the church, his salary should come from the church.)

The congregation will elect a search committee of three to five members to begin looking for a pastor. This committee will be open to suggestions from members about the kind of pastor they want.

There are different places a search committee may begin looking for a new pastor. The most obvious are Bible schools, seminaries, and churches where pastors may be interested in transferring to a new area.

The committee may get information about a prospective pastor by talking to his professors, fellow students, fellow church members, and church leaders who have worked with him.

There are some specific things the committee will want to learn about a prospective pastor.

• Does he have a burning **desire to preach**? (If he has been in seminary for three years without showing a strong urgency to preach on a regular basis, he may not have an increased sense of urgency after graduation.)

- Is he a **soul-winner**? Does he witness regularly?
- Is his **moral reputation** good?
- Does he **pay his debts?**
- Is he a **hard worker**?
- Does he believe the **Bible to be the Word of God?**
- Does he preach the Word with **authority?**
- Does he have a **clear conversion experience**?
- Does he have a **clear call of God to preach**?
- Does he **tithe**?

The committee will need to talk to a number of people and to the preacher in order to get all this information.

The committee should seek to hear a prospective pastor preach at least one time. If the committee is favorably impressed, he could be invited to preach at their church. If the preacher is married, it is important that his family attend the services when he preaches. It is best if arrangements can be made for him to preach two times on Sunday. A special time of fellowship, such as a noon meal on Sunday where all the members attend, can be helpful to get to know the prospective pastor. Church members should be given the opportunity to ask questions.

The committee may desire to have a brief meeting with the prospective pastor to discuss such things as doctrine, salary, allowances, expectations, responsibilities, etc.

A special meeting may be scheduled on the following Sunday for the church to share their feelings. The search committee may share their findings and present a recommendation. The church will vote whether to invite him. Voting is often done by secret balloting, each member simply writing a "yes" or "no" on a paper. (Secret balloting usually will give members the opportunity to vote according to the way they really feel instead of the way they think they are expected to vote.)

It is desirable that the vote be near unanimous. It would seem unwise for a pastor to accept an invitation if the vote was only 51% yes and 49% no. The church may decide that two thirds or more must be yes before extending an invitation. The church faces a great responsibility when asking a man to lead them. Much prayer and study must precede the search for the right man and the calling of the man to be the pastor.

Chapter 29

What Titles Do We Use When Referring to Religious Leaders?

This is a common question when a new church is planted. Sometimes the planter teaches so well by example that there is no need of the question arising. It is important that what is being taught is Biblical and enhances the life of the church.

There are a number of things to keep in mind at this point, one of which is Biblical teachings about religious titles. Another major area of concern is how it affects church planting and church growth. First we will note what the Bible says on this subject.

In Matthew's gospel, Jesus was talking to the crowds and to his disciples about the religious leaders of the day. He said, *They do everything so that people will see them. . . . They love the best places at feasts and the reserved seats in the synagogues; they love to be greeted with respect in the marketplaces and to have people call them 'Teacher.' You must not be called 'Teacher,' because you are all brothers of one another and have only one Teacher. And you must not call anyone here on earth 'Father,' because you have only one Father in heaven. Nor should you be called 'Leader,' because your one and only leader is the Messiah. The greatest one among you must be your servant. Whoever makes himself great will be humbled, and whoever humbles himself will be made great.* Matthew 23:5-12

Well meaning Protestants and evangelicals often are guilty of disregarding the words of Christ found in Matthew 23. Jesus is clearly speaking against the use of religious titles. It is wrong to call a religious leader, **father, reverend, bishop, cardinal, pastor,** or any other title unduly magnifying a person. Man is not to be glorified. Only Christ is worthy of our exaltation. This does not mean we do not respect religious leaders. We are to respect them as well as every other brother and sister in the faith.

People who demand respect and a special recognition are to be pitied. Their spirit is not that of Christ.

The work of the pastor is a God-given task and believers are to recognize that God has called certain men to do the work of the pastor. We are not to minimize this work, but the pastor should not be elevated above the church members by the use of titles.

In addition to the words of Jesus, what does the Bible say about the use of titles for religious leaders?

Brother was the term used in the New Testament when referring to other believers.

After Paul had been converted he was referred to as Brother. In Acts 9:17 we read, *So Ananias went, entered the house where Saul was, and placed hands on him. "Brother Saul," he said, "the Lord has sent me—Jesus himself . . .*

Paul thought of himself as a brother to other followers of Christ. In I Corinthians 3:1, Paul says, *As a matter of fact, my brothers, . . .* He was writing to the believers in Corinth. Again he says in I Corinthians 14:6, *So when I come to you, my brothers . . .* In Philippians 2:29, Paul says concerning someone he is sending to the believers at Philippi, *Receive him, then, with joy, as a brother in the Lord. Show respect to all such people as he, . . .*

Throughout Paul's writings he uses the word "brother" to refer to other believers. Paul himself was never addressed with a religious title. In the Bible he is never called "Father Paul," or "Reverend Paul."

None of the disciples of Jesus used religious titles attached to their names. Can you imagine Jesus writing his name as "Father Jesus," or "Reverend Jesus?" James was the pastor of the church is Jerusalem, but we do not read "Reverend James" in the Bible.

It is enough to say that the Bible does not teach or encourage the use of special titles for believers. Jesus spoke against it.

Why is this important? How does it affect church planting?

When Jesus made an issue of religious titles in Matthew 23, He knew the danger of the use of such titles. A close study of that chapter will reveal what the dangers are. Jesus talked about the **superiority feeling** of those who enjoyed being called "Father" etc. He saw the danger of **pride** that comes when a man begins to magnify himself by having people address him with special titles. He saw the danger of religious leaders **losing touch with** the common person's life. This often happens when there is a gap between the leaders and the members. This gap is made greater when one person is elevated so high above the common people.

In church planting a worthy goal is that every member of the church be an active, full-time priest or minister (not pastor). If the church is to be strong, alive, and meaningful, it must be built upon this kind of theological bedrock. In a church where the professional minister dominates, very little is expected of the members. So every effort must be made to get away from the ecclesiastical caste system so common today. "**Everybody is somebody**" should be a theme in the church body. Proper use of titles can affect the outcome of how roles and responsibilities are accepted. Religious titles tend to create unnecessary attitudes, gaps, and barriers.

The use of Brother in the New Testament and today.

Religious leaders in the New Testament used this term to refer to other believers. There was no danger in using the term because it tells of a special relationship between believers which is made possible because of Jesus Christ.

Today, when we use the title "Brother," it describes a special relationship between two believers. This special relationship is not something brought about by the goodness or accomplishments of the believers. There is nothing of which to boast except for the new nature made possible by faith in Christ. So when believers call each other "Brother," it speaks of a relationship, and praise immediately goes to Jesus Christ, the source of the relationship.

For the one who understands this, there is no higher honor or respect—because we live to glorify Christ. To be addressed as Pastor or Father or Reverend is a great insult to a person who chooses only to glorify Christ.

You may say, "This is cultural." The believer should not live according to standards in the culture; rather he should live by the standards of the Word of God.

What should the pastor be called?

If you are among believers, you call him by name or "Brother _____."

If you are among unbelievers, you may choose to call him "Mr. _____." (Only believers will understand and appreciate the Biblical term, "Brother." To use it among unbelievers is meaningless. Around the world "Mr." is an acceptable secular title of respect.) If you are to introduce your pastor to a group of believers you could say, "I introduce to you Brother Juan Reyes, who is doing the work of the pastor at the _____Church."

This introduction reveals a special relationship that magnifies Christ, yet reveals and magnifies the gift of doing the work of a pastor.

If you introduce your pastor to a group of unbelievers you would say, "May I introduce Mr. Juan Reyes, who is the pastor of _____Church."

Conclusion.

If we follow the Bible we will ignore man-made religious pedestals and will not use religious titles. Hierarchies have no place in New Testament Christian religion. Such hierarchies have arisen when religious leaders demand high positions of praise that lead to uncontrolled power and the amassing of wealth at the expense of ordinary people.

It is a joy to see a spiritual giant, a set-aside man, called to pastoral duties, yet humble enough that he does not demand special recognition. This man is truly free in Christ.

Chapter 30

What Should We Do When There Is an Emergency Need Within the Church Family?

Soon after the birth of a church, there will arise the problem of how to deal with emergency needs within the body and from without. This is a common problem in all countries and perhaps is magnified in underdeveloped nations and communities. Many new churches have a haphazard program or no program at all to address these needs. The way a church handles such situations will either weaken or strengthen the witness of the church body. There are constructive ways which will be beneficial to all. We will look at one simple method which can easily be implemented in any church. Examples of such needs are:

• A family does not have enough money to buy medicine for a sick child.

• A family has a death and there are extra expenses which they cannot bear.

• The house of one of the families burns.

• A typhoon badly damages a house of a member.

• Non-church members come to the pastor for financial assistance.

• Beggars or swindlers come to the pastor or members telling stories of financial problems and asking for help. (Sometimes these may be genuine, but often they are professionals in securing money from person after person.)

Often people go to the pastor, thinking that he can easily get money for them. The pastor does not have money to give to meet everyone's needs. If he gives to one church member but cannot give to another, he may be criticized by the people for playing favorites.

Sometimes there are a few families in the church who may appear to have more money than others and people make it a habit to seek these families out in times of crisis. This puts an unfair burden on a few families.

What is the church to do? Are they to turn their backs on everyone and refuse to help? This is not the Christian attitude toward people in need. There should be a system which is workable for the church family and which is fair for all.

Consider the following:

Church members must recognize that when they join the group, they become part of a family. Membership in the family carries with it certain privileges and certain responsibilities. When one member of the family hurts, the whole family should be aware of it and feel a responsibility to help when needed. The church as a Family loves each member of the body and will show it, especially in times of great need.

The crisis or emergency of one family is not the sole responsibility of the pastor or one of the families of the church. It is the responsibility of the whole body, the church.

The person who is really a child of God will be slow to ask for help. God's people have a sense of dignity unknown to those not born again. People should do their very best to meet their own needs from within their immediate family. This is where responsibility begins. If needs cannot be met by the biological family, then a person may want to go to the larger family, the church. The church family should be sensitive enough to needs within the membership that the church would take the initiative and not require that a member ask for help.

A suggested church organization to help meet needs:

1. Elect a Benevolence Committee.

This could be done at the regular annual election of church officers, teachers, committees, etc. The committee would serve for one year like most of the other committees and a new committee would be elected each year. (If the church has a constitution and by-laws, this committee would fall within its guidelines on committees.)

This committee could have 3-5 members. Committee members should be faithful in the activities of the church. They should be wise and spiritually mature. As in Acts 6:2, it may be best if the pastor is spared the responsibility of being a member of this committee.

2. Everyone seeking assistance must meet with this committee before the need is presented to the church.

3. The committee should study the need and make recommendations to the church. The committee will not have authority to grant the request of anyone seeking help. It will hear the needs as presented by the person or family. After a careful and prayerful study of the request, the committee will make its recommendation to the church, either at a regular business meeting or at a special, called meeting.

4. The church, upon hearing the recommendation of the benevolence committee, will make the decision to help or not to help. The church is not forced to follow the recommendation of the committee. When the committee reports to the church, those seeking help should be present when their request is presented. But there should be a time when they are asked to leave so the members can discuss more openly the request and make the final decision without the requesting family present.

5. There may be some requests which need not be presented to the entire church. These requests are those that the committee is sure are from false needs or from professional beggars, etc. Most people with false requests would not want to come before a committee to discuss their needs.

This simple system makes it easier for the church to really be a loving family, helping those who really need help. It allows for all the church to participate in helping those in need. The money to meet the needs will come from the church funds or from a special love offering given by the members. It removes from the pastor the burden of deciding who should be helped, how much to give, and where to find the resources.

What is the pastor to do when someone comes to him asking for financial assistance? He should be instructed by the church to refer such persons to the benevolence committee. The pastor should not by-pass the committee and take the request directly to the church.

The responsibility of this committee should be well known by all the church members. All church members should be well aware of the steps necessary to obtain special assistance in times of crisis or emergency.

Chapter 31

How Can a Church Encourage Members to Reach the Lost?

(Every-Member-Evangelism in the New Church)

It is very important that the new church **be** and **do** certain things. In addition to communion with the Father and feasting on His Word, the body must be involved in sharing the Good News with others. In my book, *Let this Mind Be in You,* the theme is developed wherein God's people are be-attituded to the extent that witness will be natural and spontaneous. We will not attempt to deal with all the issues involved in personal soul-winning at this point; rather we will look at a simple method and tool which can easily be used by every member of the church. So many do not share Christ because they think it is necessary to be a professionally trained speaker or have super gifts. There are shy Christians who do not feel qualified to witness. Perhaps the problem is not shyness as much as a lack of motivation and love. Motivation and love are the necessary qualifications to be a witness. But can we remove some stumbling stones and excuses? Can we make it easier? Can we expect every believer to witness and win others to Christ? Yes, I believe this is possible.

Let us look at a simple and universally, usable program.

Outreach Bible Studies

This program will help motivated believers to be engaged in evangelism, either in group settings, or one-on-one.

Every member, no matter how shy, can use the "tools" which he has just gone through—*Good News For You* and *I Have Been Born Again, What Next?* He will use them in the same way they were used in the church planting Bible study. The power of positive expectation becomes an issue again. The leader must believe that every member can lead someone else to faith in Christ. If a child is old enough to understand how to be saved, he is old enough to lead someone else to Christ, but we must expect it and be willing to help. I believe it is within reason to expect every member to lead at least one person to Christ every year.

THE FOLLOWING SIMPLE STRUCTURE MAY BE ADEQUATE.

An outreach co-ordinator should be elected by the church.

Directors of Outreach Bible Studies will also be elected by the church. A larger church will need secretarial help to assist in this program of outreach.

These officers could be elected when the church elects other officers. The success will depend heavily upon these leaders. They must believe that every member should and can win at least one person to Christ each year.

There are two general areas of outreach, **Community Bible Studies** and **Personal Bible Studies.**

The community Bible study has a wider range of participants while the personal may be a one-on-one Bible study. Each member of the church should be expected to be involved in one or both.

I. Duties of the Director of Community Bible Studies

1. General survey and analysis of community
2. Enlist leaders
3. Train leaders
4. Co-ordinate groups and materials
5. Monitor groups and total program
6. Keep records
7. Relate groups to church
8. Promote outreach program

Duties of the Leaders of the Community Bible Studies

1. Determine place/date/time for the Bible Study
2. Enlist class members
3. Secure materials from the director
4. Guide the Bible Study
5. Relate the group to church

II. Duties of the Director of Personal Bible Studies

1. Secure list of church membership
2. Secure commitment of every member. The pastor and other leaders must be totally supportive of expectation levels.
3. Equip members to be motivated to use what they already know
4. Lead each member to pray that the Holy Spirit will lead to a responsive person
5. Keep records of each member and enrollee/s
6. Make available needed Bible study material
7. Have celebration rallies when helpful for encouragement and drawing new converts into the church
8. Develop a system to allow for progress reports

No limit need be put on the number of community Bible studies. The goal is to saturate the community and beyond with a prolonged exposure to the Good News of salvation as found in the Word of God. If the unbeliever is guided through the seven *Good News For You* lessons and does not make a decision to follow Christ, the believer is expected to find someone else and keep up the process until he has led at least one person to Christ within the year. (We will not discourage a person if he gets excited and wins several to Christ in the year.)

Nothing will revolutionize a church more than for every member to annually lead at least one person to Christ. It is possible, and the best time to start is when the new church is planted. Do not wait until they find out it is "acceptable" to go a lifetime and never lead anyone to Christ.

SECTION VI

THE CHURCHES IN FELLOWSHIP

Chapter 32

The Birth of a Fellowship or Association

Objective three: Establishing an Indigenous Association of Churches

Some people are afraid of "fellowships" or "associations" and rightfully so if any church's autonomy is violated by any such organization. No association of churches should ever have control over a local church. Some associations hold this principle high in word, yet in action exert unhealthy control over churches. Pastors tell of how they are "blackballed" if they do not back the association program to the letter. They are considered uncooperative if they do not choose to participate in every program handed down by a convention or association. This kind of underhanded control is not worthy of the name of Christianity. Each association is autonomous, never under the control of a larger external body, and the church is just as autonomous. Each church in a fellowship of churches has its own personality and program to meet specific needs of its members. Just as one will find power struggles gradually developing in most churches, this will also be a tendency for the association of churches. The planter can help head this off with a strong emphasis that "everybody is somebody," teaching the concept of servanthood in word and deed.

Some church planters will be working in pioneering areas where there is no fellowship or association of churches. Others will be working in areas where other churches are already in existence.

◆ In Pioneer Areas

It was Paul's ambition to plant churches in unevangelized and unchurched areas. In Romans 15:20 he said, *My ambition has always been to proclaim the Good News in places where Christ has not been heard of, so as not to build on a foundation laid by someone else.* There is a greater freedom for the planter in such circumstances. This is especially true if he wants to plant indigenous churches.

No planter should feel satisfied just to get a church planted. There is a need for encouragement and sharing beyond that which the planter can do. Churches need sister churches. As a church planter, I am well aware of my objectives long before beginning the first Bible study.

Those objectives include:

- The salvation of individuals
- The birth of indigenous churches
- The birth of an indigenous association of churches

After the third and final objective has been reached, I am free to go to another area and start the process all over again. People ask me how long it takes to plant an indigenous association of churches. It depends on the responsiveness of the people. In some places it may take many years and in other places only a few years. When I speak of having led in the establishment of an association to the point of being ready to transfer to another place, I am thinking of at least ten to fifteen churches. This many may not be required, but there is strength in numbers. The greater the number of churches, the easier it will be for them to employ their own national coordinator for the work.

This person may be called a church planter, director of missions, associational missionary, or a combination of any of these. If the association is to be purely indigenous, the churches will pay the salary of this person.

If the planter is aware of the third objective he will remember that the proximity of newly established churches will make a difference in reaching it. If the churches are scattered over a very wide geographical area, it will be more difficult to develop association between the churches. So it may be wise to think in terms of planting a group of churches within a short distance of each other. This will affect the future ability of the churches to encourage each other. Though the planter is aware of this dynamic, he will go where the Holy Spirit leads him no matter what the distance.

Where do we begin? After a church is born the members are made aware of ongoing Bible studies in nearby places. There will be a rejoicing when the next new church is born. After the birth of three or four churches, the planter may suggest to each of the churches the possibility of a joint meeting. Usually each new church will be very happy to get to know fellow believers from other locations. The planter may suggest a Saturday morning meeting at a central location. The first meetings will be very informal. The earliest needs of the churches are:

- Fellowship
- Encouragement
- Sharing
- Inspiration

In much of the world there is persecution of some degree facing new converts who take a serious stand for Christ. Often this persecution involves the family, finances, and profession. The newly formed core group of each church finds refuge in the local church family. But churches can encourage churches. The birth of an association should not come about just because it is the pattern in another part of the country or world; it should evolve out of real needs.

The first associational meeting should not focus on organization. That will come as needed. It is strange and artificial to give primary attention to election of officers in the beginning. Often election of officers is followed with hours devoted to developing a long list of policies and guidelines. These may not be bad, but they are not usually the first things needed. To get entangled with such legalistic affairs may set the pace for future emphases. Sometimes such developments lead to an association of pastors and a few church leaders.

Remember that an association of churches means:

1. Associating, fellowshipping, sharing
2. Church members from various churches, not just pastors and leaders

The practiced motto **"the church where everybody is somebody"** is very vital to the well-being of the local church. Even so the motto **"the fellowship where everybody is somebody"** is vital to healthy growth. What do you do when the churches first begin to come together for fellowship meetings? First, involve every church in some way. There should be a time of recognition of each church. I have always assumed that each church would present special music. This is one area where any church can easily take part. If the meeting is a half day on Saturday, most all of the church leaders/pastors can share in some way. This may include testimonies, Scripture reading, leading in prayer, or preaching.

In some places, snacks or bringing your own lunch may present an ideal time for fellowship. The planter will not need to baby the people at this point. The planter will be a participant. Let the people be responsible, no matter how poor economically they may be. They will provide what they are accustomed to if they are expected to.

Decisions which need to be made by the churches at the first fellowship meeting:

1. How often to meet

I have found quarterly meetings to be effective. Special pastors/workers meetings would be in addition to these fellowship meetings. (I choose to call the early meetings fellowship meetings because that is basically what they are and where I want to focus.) The day of the week when the meeting is held is critical. If it is to be an association of pastors, a week day could be chosen. But since our desire is an association of churches, a day should be chosen when it is easiest for church members to attend. This may be Saturday or Sunday. Sunday may be too full with local church activities.

2. Where to meet each time

If the churches are scattered, it is usually best to meet at a central location if possible. One of the best ways to kill an association of churches is to have meetings in far away, hard-to-get-to places. If this is done, the association of churches will degenerate into an association of pastors and workers. Sometimes, out of a desire to be nice, an unthinking brother will invite the churches to come to his place. It may be difficult for the churches to say no for fear of hurting feelings. This is where wise leadership can be exerted by the church planter. He can make suggestions and give the reasons why the central place is usually better. So it may be best not to ask volunteers to host the next meeting. The central location is crucial; it simply makes it easier for the church members to attend. If the distance is too great, it may be too expensive and time consuming for some to make the trip.

Since this is a new thing for the churches, the experienced church planter will want to be in charge of the first associational meetings. He will have to plan the theme and program. But this is only to be done in the early stages of the association. As soon as possible, others should begin participating in every stage of the planning.

The church planter will need to educate the churches about the concept of a fellowship. They will have to be educated about each step that is to be taken in the establishment of a board of directors and any other boards or committees.

Every country may have their own distinct association structure. The following is an example only.

ASSOCIATIONAL BOARD OF DIRECTORS

Each church will elect three board members.

The board members should be elected each year by individual churches. A board member should be reelected only if he has taken his position seriously the previous year. If a member fails to continue meeting any of the following qualifications, he/she should not be reelected. The pastor may serve on the board if elected.

Qualifications of board members:

• Active member of local church

- Morally upright
- Sound in Christian doctrine
- Able to attend associational meetings
- Respected and considered spiritually mature by the church

Time of board meetings:

It may be best to have board meetings immediately following quarterly fellowship meetings in order to save extra meetings.

Duties of the board:

The board will ultimately deal with all matters of the association. There will be other committees and study bodies, but primary authority will lie with the board. The board may be the only body elected by the churches. It is important to keep authority in the hands of the churches, and it is the churches who will give authority to the board. The church planter should be a member of the board. Some of the duties include:

1. Approving by-laws and constitution of the association;
2. Making decisions concerning receiving new churches into the association;
3. Approving employment of personnel such as local church planters and coordinator of the work;
4 Approving special projects.

EXECUTIVE COMMITTEE

This committee is elected by the board of directors at the January meeting. It may consist of three to five members. The qualifications of those serving on this committee will be the same as for board members. Executive committee members may be serving on the board, but others should be considered also. No church should have more than one member on the executive committee. If the geographical area is large, it may be best to have representation from different areas.

Chairman of Executive Committee

The executive committee will elect their chairman as the first item of business at the first meeting of the new committee. The chairman may serve as moderator of the fellowship meetings.

Duties of executive committee

1. Give general direction to work of association
2. Make recommendations to the association board of directors
3. Plan association meetings
4. Serve as strategy committee
5. Make necessary decisions during times when the board is not meeting. If there are decisions of great consequence, the board should be called into emergency session.
6. Serve as advisory committee
7. Develop association budget to be presented to the board
8. Serve as personnel committee

Time of meetings for the executive committee

If the association fellowships are held in January, April, July, and October, the executive committee may want to meet six weeks following each of the quarterly meetings. These would be the regular meetings and special meetings could be called as needed.

The church planter should be an ex-officio member of the executive committee. He should not dominate the committee. If the church planter is a foreigner, special restraint will be necessary to keep from making all the decisions or overly influencing the committee.

The structure of the association should be simple. Each part of the structure should evolve gradually from real and felt needs by the churches. In the early stages, there will be no need for a special office or a lot of equipment. When these needs develop, the churches of the association should be the ones to make such provisions. If it is theirs, they will take pride in it and maintain it. If the idea and the funding come from a foreigner, the churches will not readily accept ownership. The churches will be resentful when the outsider decides it is time for them to take full responsibility for direction and maintenance.

Annual camps

This may be an early program of the new association of churches. Camps for youth are common around the world and their value is obvious. Permit the association to decide the place, time, and eventually the program of the camps.

◆ In Areas With Established Work

The second possible scenario in which the church planter may find himself is a place where a few churches have already been established. Planting indigenous churches in such an area will not be a big problem if the older churches have been established on indigenous principles. This, however, may not be the case. In most conferences I have conducted, there are several present who are facing real struggles at this point. It is very difficult to plant indigenous churches in an area where there are established non-indigenous churches. Most planters come to the conclusion that the two just don't mix.

So what is one to do if he finds himself in such a situation?

Be loving, courteous, and an encourager to the established churches. Be available to work with them on a limited basis.

Very often non-indigenous churches will take as much attention, time, and money as you will give them. Non-indigenous churches may tend to have lazy leadership who will want you to preach for them as often as possible. They also know the more often a foreigner is with them, the more money they are apt to get.

In my first church planting assignment, I found myself in a situation like this. For one year I tried to work with two or three established churches. It became apparent that they had been totally debilitated by a continuous parental relationship. Dignity and self-worth had long been gone. I realized that if churches with dignity and selfhood in Christ were to be planted, it would be necessary to start fresh church-planting Bible studies. I remained a friend to the older churches, but new churches were started. The new churches began to have quarterly fellowships. After a few fellowship meetings, I subtly let the older churches know of the meetings, without strong encouragement to attend. I did not want to leave them completely out of the picture. One of these churches attended and there was the usual sharing of how God was blessing. A member of the non-indigenous church was visiting with a member of a new indigenous church. The member from the non-indigenous church told how the mission had given them land, a building, and a pastor's salary for five years. In no time the member from the young church came to me and asked why the mission had done that for them and had not done it for the new churches.

My response was, "But they were not strong like you are; you do not have to be dependent on outside help because you are strong. God is your source. He is so much better than an American." I would emphasize the strength of one and the weakness of the other. In time the indigenous church members began to feel sorry for the churches who had become dependent on outside help.

After we had spent seven years in that province and had left to go to another place to start the process all over again, we received a letter from the national church planter/coordinator of the work. The conclusion drawn was this: "I have tried so hard to bring the old established churches into the association and I have come to the conclusion it may be impossible. It is like mixing oil with water."

A word of caution: If you find yourself in such a situation, I strongly suggest you go ahead and do your thing in planting New Testament indigenous churches, but do it quietly. Do not boast that you are doing something different. Do it and let the fruits speak for themselves. Effective and lasting fruit will gain you credibility. This low profile is important not only among the churches, but also among missionaries. If you are working in a mission where foreign aid has bought disciples and churches for years, you will not be popular if you seek to plant churches who are not dependent on the mission. Someone will say you are planting "independent churches." The lesson has been deeply imbedded that if you do not finance a situation, it may get out of your control. As a planter of indigenous churches, your primary objective is a body of believers dependent only on Christ as head and source. So, do it and do it quietly and watch the fruit reveal its viability and worthiness.

The Church Planter in Relation to the Individual Churches

If a church planter has planted several churches, where should he have his church membership? I have found that all the churches I start assume that I am a part of their body, even though I do not formally join the church. A number of factors influence the place of my membership. The proximity of my home may make a difference. If I live close to a particular church, I may want to be a member there. If there is a key "mother church" that was started first, this may be the logical place for me to be a member. In some developing nations, some pastors will want you to be a member in their church so you will feel obligated to put your tithes there. This attitude is not normally seen among churches with indigenous principles. It often will be seen among churches who have their hand out each time you arrive in effect saying, "What do you have for us today?"

Although the planter may officially be a member of one church, he will need to give adequate attention to each of the new churches. To do this he may want to set up a rotation schedule to be with each church on a regular basis. New churches will not need his leadership in the worship services, but they will need to know that he cares about and loves them, even beyond their birth.

This leads to another question: Where will the church planter put his tithe? If he comes from an industrialized nation and is working in an undeveloped country, his salary may be much higher than that of the members of the newly-formed churches. What is the planter to do if his income greatly exceeds that of the people he is working among? If he gives all his tithe to the new church, there will be more money than needed and the members will not need to give any. In the beginning, the planter must find other places for most of his tithe. This may be to another church, to a convention, missions, or other outreach programs. Some will argue "storehouse tithing" and I understand this principle, but giving a large tithe to a baby church made up of low income folks will tend to be a greater hindrance than help. After a number of churches have been started and an association program has been started, there will be places the planter can distribute his tithe in a constructive way.

An indigenous association is functioning on its own. Now what?

Once the church planter's third objective—the birth of an indigenous association of churches—has been reached, he will go to another area and start over again.

If the planter should continue to work in the area, he will not sever relationships with the association. He must, however, be very sensitive so as not to undermine or intimidate the newly elected leaders. He will continue as a Christian brother and as a co-laborer. He may offer encouragement, but he should function strictly as a church planter, working within the structure of the association. If he is a foreigner, it may be very important not to serve on important committees. Many Americans find it difficult not to be overly dominant in decision making. Many believers in third-world countries lack adequate self-esteem to go against an opinion of a person from an industrialized nation.

There is no greater joy than seeing healthy, indigenous associations started which go on to do far greater things than they were able to do under the leadership of the original church planter. To plant such an association is a worthy objective.

What about a convention?

I am confident that a large body of churches can do more cooperatively than any one church. Therefore, for purposes of joint ventures such as missions and theological education, there is a need for a larger fellowship made up of more than one association. Sometimes this larger body is called a "fellowship" or convention of churches. Again, the same principle of autonomy is true here as in the case of the smaller local association. No convention body should ever have control over a local church or association. Churches are free to voluntarily cooperate with other churches which make up a convention of churches. No convention should ever intimidate local churches to automatically follow their programs.

There are some religious bodies that have developed an imprimatur on literature used. If a particular church does not use literature produced by that religious body, the church may be considered uncooperative and suspect. This is not the direction that leads to healthy, autonomous churches. This is undesirable external control. There is a real danger of power struggles in a convention; this is only possible when servanthood takes a back seat to politics. In spite of the inherent dangers of unhealthy dynamics within a body of people, the body—small or large—is still the way to go. No one can stand alone and be Christian at the same time, there must be a vertical relationship to God and a horizontal relationships to others. The church, the association of churches, the convention of churches must keep Christ and His purpose at the center of every attitude and action. The church planter will be involved in it all and it can be a beautiful journey.

APPENDIX

A normal process in the church-planting experience of Charles Brock when working among responsive people

	7 weeks	11 weeks	Bible Study continues	6 weeks	21 weeks	16 weeks	Special denominational programs are introduced upon their ability to meet the needs of each particular group. The Bible is the basic text in member nurturing and in leadership training.
I n t r o duction	*Good News for You* by Charles Brock	*I Have Been Born Again, What Next?* by Charles Brock	Worship services led by members	*Galatians* by Charles Brock	*John* by Charles Brock	*Romans* by Charles Brock	
	Salvation	Pre-chruch	Baptism and birth of a church (18-21 weeks)	Chapter by chapter through Galatians, John, and Romans. Study guides designed for new leaders are available for each book.			

Formal Leadership Training Begins	**Level 1:** **Emphasis on functional** * The worship service * The work of a pastor * *Questions People and Churches Ask* by Charles Brock * Intro. to Bible wintessing * Church planting Often it is most logical for the planter to lead in this training program, especially if he is in pioneering areas.	**Level 2:** *Let This Mind Be in You* by Charles Brock * Preaching * Work of pastor * Bible interpretation * TEE (Theological Education by Extension) * *Questions People and Churches Ask*, by Charles Brock The *Questions* book continues to serve as a resource and is of value for new churches and believers who for some reason lose contact with church planters.
Church Member Bible Studies	Sunday School, Christian Training, etc. Director is chosen by the church. Bible reading report time is set when most convenient. For a new church the hour before the worship often is best. All members participate. (See pp 9, 204 in *Questions People and Churches Ask*, Brock)	
Every Member Evangelism	Director of community Bible studies elected by church. Bible Study Leaders: *Good News for You* is used as it was in beginning the church. New converts are introduced to the church and enrolled in *I Have Been Born Again, What Next?*	

MY TESTIMONY

Name _____
Date _____

Your testimony is the experience you had with Christ when you were born again. Tell it in simple, easy to understand words.

1. My life before accepting Christ as my personal Savior and Lord.

2. What happened to make me realize my need of Jesus?

3. What I did to be saved.

4. How my life has changed since that day.

Month _____ Year _____ Name _____

Calendar for Personal Bible Reading

Source (name of book)	Sun.	Mon.	Tues.	Wed.	Thur.	Fri.	Sat.	Weekly Totals (chapters)
_____								
_____								
_____								
_____								
_____								

Total chapters read for month _____

Verses that had special meaning to me this week:

Week 1 _____

Week 2 _____

Week 3 _____

Week 4 _____

Step 1: On the calendar place number of day in blank. (A commercial calendar or diary also works well.)

Step 2: Choose a book from the Bible to read. (Stay with one book until it is finished and then choose another.)

Step 3: Plan to read more than one chapter each day. (If you read three chapters daily you will read through the Bible in one year.)

Step 4: Each day write on the calendar the number of chapters you read that day.

Step 5: At the end of each week write the total chapters you read that week.

Step 6: Day by day write down the chapters and verses that spoke to you in a special way.

Step 7: You will report to the group once a week. The report will include:
A. The book you read B. Total chapters read C. You will read some of the verses that spoke to you in a special way. (You will not interpret or try to explain the verse — just read it.) Give book, chapter and verse and allow time for members to find it in their Bibles.

Step 8: It will be helpful if you will buy a small notebook to use in taking daily notes as you read.

Step 9: It will also help to obtain color markers or light green or yellow crayons to highlight special verses.

Report Time: at one of the regular group meetings each week. Reports should be brief enough to allow all members to report.

CHURCH GROWTH DEFINITIONS
(From a paper prepared by Jim Slack)

I. A Definition of Church Growth.

"We are to preach the message of God to every creature in such a way that regenerated converts will result. These will form local churches, established according to the New Testament pattern and operating as self-sustaining and self-propagating units, to the end that vital churches will multiply in every area of the world." (CG & CM : 1965 p. 217)

". . . **church growth**—namely the conversions of persons to God and the planting of churches or fellowships . . ." (CG & CM : 1983 p. 49)

II. Definitions of common Church Growth Terms.

The terms listed below are common terms that one who studies, practices, and talks about church growth should be familiar with because they are often used.

1. **Eurica** or **Eurican** - Europe and North America

2. **Afericasia** - Africa, Latin America, and Asia

3. **Search Theology** - A theology of seed sowing, which means that in Christian mission the essential thing is not the finding but going everywhere and preaching the Gospel. The proclamation of Christ by word and deed whether men hear or not, whether they obey or not.

4. **Harvest Theology** - Christians should win the winnable while they are winnable. Draws this basically from Matthew 9:37 where Jesus instructed His disciples to pray that God would send laborers into the harvest and the passage that teaches the disciples to choose the responsive over the resistant people. Seeing the responsiveness of a particular population, our Lord recognized the need for reapers.

5. **Receptive Population** - Those who readily accept the Gospel and are "winnable" to the Lord now.

6. **Resistant Population** - Those which do not accept or those who are resistant to the preaching of the Gospel. Places, areas, groups, etc., that show little response to the Gospel.

7. **Universal Fog** - A general haziness and often reluctance, or perhaps ignorant indifference toward ascertaining exactly, statistically, qualitatively, or measuring in other ways, what has been done in the past in the area of church growth. This includes what they have done, what they are now doing, and what they do or do not plan to do in the future.

8. **Cultural Overhang** - The tendency of men to see everything in their own cultural frame of reference. Included here would be the thinking that what works in one place will work in other places. This includes methods of evangelism, denominational structures, and other church practices which may be used in one country successfully. Assuming they will work in all places is Cultural Overhang.

9. **Homogeneous Unit** - A section of society, a group, a language group, an ethnic group such as a tribal group, a racial group, etc., or other groups, in which all members of the group have some common characteristics. Student groups, sections of towns, country, professional groups, slum areas, etc., might all be homogeneous units.

10. **Biological Church Growth** - Church growth derived only from those born into Christian families.

11. **Transfer Church Growth** - The increase of one congregation by accepting one who transfers his membership from another congregation.

12. **Conversion Church Growth** - Those outside the Church (and the Church must be defined to distinguish this type of growth from transfer type) that come to accept Christ and are baptized and "added to the Lord" in His Church.

13. **Full Families** - A case where the husband and wife are Christians.

14. **Half Families** - A case where only one partner is Christian.

15. **Masses** - The larger part of a society, usually the laboring class, whose income is usually low, where education is usually lower and where the living conditions are usually very poor in quality. In the Philippines we call this the "Bakya" crowd.

16. **Classes** - This is the dividing of society into groups, categories, or sections, according to economics, living conditions, attainment, etc. Basically, a group of people

having common characteristics. This is very similar to the Homogenous Unit. The difference is that the classes category is not geographically limited as homogeneous unit.

17. **People Movements** - This is where a tribe, a caste, or any homogeneous unit moves into Christianity. "People become Christian as a wave of decisions for Christ sweeps through the group mind, involving many individual decisions but being far more than merely their sum. This may be called a chain reaction. Each decision sets off others and the sum total powerfully affects every individual." (McGavran in *The Bridges of God*) A people movement therefore results from the joint decision of a number of individuals, all from the same people, which enables them to become Christians without social dislocation, while remaining in full contact with their non-Christian relatives.

18. **One-by-One-Mode** - Winning individuals to Christ, one by one.

19. **Multi-Individual Conversion** - A situation where many people participate in the act of deciding for Christ. Each individual makes up his own mind and if he believes, then he joins those who are becoming Christians.

20. **Mutually Interdependent** - Conversions in which those making the decisions are intimately known to each other and take the step in view of what the other is going to do.

21. **Multi-Individual, Mutually Interdependent Conversion** - A group has decided for Christ, in which each individual was saved, not by going along with the crowd, but by his participation in the decision.

22. **Lyddic Movements** - A type of people movement in which the entire community becomes Christian. (Taken from the word Lydda and place Lydda in Acts 9.)

23. **Lystran Movement** - A type of people movement in which the entire community becomes Christian and the balance becomes hostile. (See Acts 14 and 16.)

24. **Laodicean Movement** - A people movement which slows down and stagnates.

25. **Ephesian Movement** - A group considers themselves as "disciples" of Christ although they knew little about Him. This is what Paul saw at Ephesus.

26. **Web Movement** - A case of extended families and is characteristic of Africasia in which every one in a small group knows his cousins, aunts, in-laws, godfathers, etc., and they are closely attached to each other. This extended family concept forms therefore a "Web" which becomes a movement when any of the influential members of the web becomes a Christian.

27. **Indigenous - Self-governing, self-supporting, and self-propagating.** Specifically, the word means "produced, growing, or living naturally in a country or climate; native." Webster.

28. **Anthropology** - The science of man. " The science of man (study of man) in relation of physical character, distribution, origin, classification and relationship of races, environmental and social relations, and culture." Webster.

29. **Urban** - Belonging to or concerning the city or town.

30. **Rural** - Belonging to or concerning the country, the province, or non-urban areas.

31. **Nevius Method** - Churches and Mission work seeks to minimize the paid national agency, and believes that the principle of independence and self-reliance, applied from the very beginning, will sooner bring about the establishment of independent, self-reliant, aggressive national churches.

32. **Communication terms used in surveys** - 1) Censors, 2) Creators, 3) Purveyors, and 4) Receivers. (Nida uses these terms often:)

    Censor - Usually the chiefs, rulers, elders, and upper-class leaders who decide whether or not a message is accepted or rejected.

    Creators - Usually not the leaders, but those competing for leadership.

    Purveyors - Those who report, such as newsmen, radio announcers, or messengers.

    Receivers - Those being influenced by the above mentioned groups.

Bible Study Materials
For Church Planting and Church Growth

Indigenous Church Planting, A Practical Journey is part of a system of church planting materials prepared by Charles Brock. This system includes the following books:

1. **Leading a Bible Study by Indirect Methods** is a simple learning exercise of programmed instruction to teach a few basic things about a method of leadership. Anyone who leads a study of the following Bible study books should first work through this lesson. It will take less than one hour.

2. **Good News for You** is a presalvation study. The purpose of these lessons based on the Gospel of John is to bring people to an authentic salvation experience.

3. **I Have Been Born Again, What Next?** is a prechurch study. These lessons are for new believers, leading them to understand Christian privileges and responsibilities in preparation for becoming responsible church members. These lessons are also good for new member orientation in established churches.

4. **Galatians, From Law to Grace,** is to be used by the leader of a new church. It is written so that a new believer can use it as a guide in the first worship services in a new church. The leader need not have special training to use the guide. It is a chapter-by-chapter study of the book of Galatians.

5. **John, Behold the Lamb** is to be used by the worship leader after the study of Galatians has been completed. The study guide for John is a chapter-by-chapter expository treatment of the text.

6. Romans, The Road to Righteousness is the third study guide to be used by the worship leader. The leader may choose to follow it closely or use it as a resource for sermon preparation.

7. Questions People and Churches Ask addresses 52 questions most often asked by new believers and new leaders. This book is designed to be used for the training of new leaders.

8. Let This Mind Be in You gives a theological foundation that under-girds indigenous church planting.

9. Principles and Practice of Indigenous Church Planting is a practical, "in-a-nutshell" guide for church planting.

10. Indigenous Church Planting In Review is a quick reference for use with "A Practical Journey" and a primer for those wanting to become church planters.

11. Good News In Song – 51 songs in a small booklet that is designed for use with *Good News For You* Bible studies.

These books may be ordered from:

Church Growth International
13174 Owens Lane
Neosho, Missouri 64850

Phone: 417-451-1648
Fax: 417-451-0367